PROJECT MANAGEMENT SIMPLY EXPLAINED

DOUGLAS C. RUH JR.

DEDICATION

This book is dedicated to my wife Glendee, without whom my life would be very different. She has supported me in this adventure and been my companion, friend and confidante throughout our life together.

CONTENTS

ACKNOWLEDGMENTS

This book is the product of a Project Management class taken at Northwest University in Kirkland, Washington. Instructor Barry Otterholt has been a Project Management Professional (PMP) in the IT business for many years, as well as an instructor on the topic. His belief and excitement about project management is evident in the classroom and his teaching style made learning about project management fun and informative.

Education, especially earning a bachelor's degree, has been a long-term goal. I have had the good fortune to have met some very fine people who have become study partners and friends. During my time at the community college I met a group of students that became my study group. All are international students and we helped each other whenever and however we could. Shufei (Sophie) and Yi Hua were the first of the group, then came Xinyue (Cindy), Azusa, Yuka, Hsin Ting (Derica), Aya and Emmanuel. I owe them much thanks for teaching me how to buckle down and study hard and to enjoy the learning process. They also have enriched the lives of me and my wife with their friendship, sharing their traditions and customs with us as we have shared ours with them. My friends and primary study group at Northwest University included Tonie, Sheila, Andrew, Chrissy and Mary principally. As a group, we seemed to bring out the best in each other, challenged one another and were always striving to produce the best work product we knew how.

CHAPTER 1
FUNDAMENTALS

Project Management is a fairly simple and straightforward concept. Decide on a project, develop and execute the project, and create a finished product. This world also can become a bit complicated with process steps, project goals, new terminology, overlapping project steps and all the rest that goes with orchestrating numerous people and resources toward a finished product. Here, in the next few pages, I will try and explain the basics in a simple, straightforward manner.

What's a Project?

A project is an effort, duty or task that is short term or temporary, has a beginning and an end point, and produces a specific, unique result.

A process is similar except that it has sustained results, it is repeated time and again, and is repetitive in nature.

An example of a project: Your child's birthday is fast-approaching. You decide to bake a birthday cake for their celebration. Baking a cake for this birthday is a one-time project. It is temporary (you are not baking them a cake every day), producing a specific, unique result. It is a project.

If you started a bakery and made cakes on a daily basis, this would be considered a process, as opposed to a birthday cake project.

What's a Stakeholder?

A Stakeholder is any person (or organization) that is actively involved in the project. Stakeholders also include individuals who are involved in and affected by the project outcome or product.

During the project process, the person(s) making the cake are Stakeholders. They are invested in making a tasty and attractive cake. The birthday girl or boy is also a Stakeholder because the cake is made for their celebration. The party attendees are Stakeholders because they will be eating cake with the celebrants. Further removed from the partygoers and the baker, it could also be said that the stores where the cake ingredients were purchased are Stakeholders, as are the businesses that supplied the ingredients.

Why Do a Project?

Projects are undertaken when results outside the ordinary course of business are needed or wanted. Projects can help to bolster performance or results by implementing a new business strategy, streamlining processes or creating a new product.

Projects create "deliverables" that are intended to have a benefit to the Stakeholders. If there were no benefit, there would be no need for a project.

What's Project Management?

Project Management is the process of managing all elements of a project, from the initiating and planning stages through the handing off of a deliverable (the product) to the customer, and the closing of the project. Project management is technically defined as "the application of knowledge, skills, tools and techniques to project activities to meet the project requirements (PMBOK®, v.4)."

When starting the cake making project, we would include Grandma, because she is an excellent baker, a great knowledge resource and a skilled artisan. We also would include her mixer, bowls, spatulas, pans and oven as tools. The ingredients wouldn't hurt the project if they also were included.

Project Management is using these resources in a manner that makes sense and is the most efficient to produce our cake.

The Project Life Cycle

Every project has a life cycle. If there is not a life cycle defined, it becomes a product, a process or a mess.

The basic project life cycle consists of a definite starting point and a definite ending point or closing point.

In between, where the work gets done are four general stages of the project.

These stages include the:

Starting Project Phase or Initiating Phase. In this phase, the idea is formed and discussed, and a general need for the project is agreed upon.

Organizing and Preparing Phase or Planning Phase. This is straightforward, and involves planning the project and activities, gathering and arranging supplies, and consulting with Stakeholders and experts to ensure the working phase has every chance for success.

Carrying out the Project Work Phase, or Execution Phase. This is the phase where the work has been decided upon, assignments and activities assigned, and a schedule completed. It's go time!

Closing the Project Phase. The deliverable (the finished project) is not the end of the project. To properly close out a project, all loose ends will need to be tied off.

The cake project's Starting Project Phase may include brainstorming the idea; gathering input on size, flavor and type of cake as well as alternatives; and deciding on the final project parameters.

Organizing and Preparing would include procuring the wet and dry ingredients; the tools, labor, oven and pans; and the instructions and intangibles like knowledge and technique.

Carrying out the Project Work Phase would include reading and following the directions, using the correct tools and ingredients to make the batter, and actually baking the cake.

Closing the Project Phase includes all the actions necessary to properly close out the project: frosting the cake and presenting it to the Stakeholders; cleaning the workplace and ensuring all tools and supplies are put back; and gaining final approval and acceptance by the Stakeholders.

The Five Standard Process Groups

A project has five standard process groups, which when combined become the process structure and roadmap, ensuring all the processes involved in the project are identified and completed.

Initiating is the first process group. This includes discussing the need for a project, if the project is feasible and would it have a benefit if it is undertaken. In the initiation phase, discussions lead to the determination that a party is just not a party without cake. This is our deliverable from the initiation phase; a cake is needed for a successful party and the project is to make a cake.

Planning is the next process group. Planning involves making lists of needs for the project. These lists include labor, knowledge, time, supplies and schedule. This is by no means an exhaustive list of items that planning entails, but the long and short of it is the planning stage is where the project takes shape and is when a roadmap for the project is constructed. Planning out our cake production would include scheduling Grandma's time and kitchen, procuring the supplies and tools, outlining specific steps to be taken, determining the order, and documenting the effort and time needed to push the project along in an efficient manner from idea to finished cake.

Executing is the third process group and includes the work performed to move the project from an idea and assembled supplies to finished product, or deliverable. This is the phase in which we get our hands dirty. Executing our cake project includes heating the oven, measuring and combining the dry and the wet ingredients, and mixing them thoroughly. This also includes preparing the pan, pouring the mixed ingredients in, inserting the pan into the oven and setting the timer to alert when the bake time is finished.

Closing the process is an important process group that defines the end of the project by delivering the project deliverables to the Sponsor or customer. In this case it is the birthday cake that is the deliverable. Delivery is not the end of the project, though. To properly close out a project, more needs to be done. In our case, the cake needs to be frosted as the final execution task. When it is frosted, then the deliverable is handed off to the closing process group. Delivering the cake is the first step. Other duties include washing the dishes and ensuring that everything is put away. Tools and utensils are properly returned. Counters are wiped clean, Grandma is relieved of her responsibility, and the garbage is taken out. Everything is returned to its expected state.

Monitor and Control group is usually mentioned last on the list but is ever present at each stage and activity in some manner. This group and process monitors and controls quality, time, resources and changes during each of the other phases. This group monitors, tracks, reviews and regulates the progress of each stage of the project. They also identify areas of change and then initiate the changes to the processes. This is Grandma.

The Ten Standard Knowledge Areas

There are ten standard knowledge areas in project management. Each area has a specific set of knowledge and involvement in the project process. The ten areas are:

Project Integration Management. Integrates and consolidates outputs from all areas to ensure a workable plan is obtained.

Project Scope Management. Output is the scope of the project. The scope keeps the project well defined and within time constraints.

Project Time Management. Manages time for each step in the project and ensures project is delivered on time.

Project Cost Management. Output details the various costs of the project including labor, materials, etc.

Project Quality Management. Assures that the quality level agreed upon is delivered.

Project Human Resources Management. Sources and maintains the correct and appropriate amount of human resources for each stage of the project.

Project Communication Management. Creates and manages communication channels between the Stakeholders.

Project Risk Management. Identifies and manages risks to the project that may occur and attempts to mitigate the risks beforehand.

Project Procurement Management. Obtains the necessary equipment and supplies involved in the project, ensuring a smooth flow of progress.

Project Stakeholder Management. Identifies Stakeholders, plans and controls Stakeholder engagement. This new knowledge area was separated out because Stakeholder communication, engagement and management is considered crucial to a project.

These knowledge areas are critical to the success of a project and are specific areas of knowledge that contribute to effectively monitoring and controlling the project schedule, communications, labor, costs and scope.

Each of the 42 project management processes will reside in one of these knowledge areas. These knowledge areas are akin to storage areas for the processes that are needed in these areas. Although the five process groups and the nine knowledge areas are listed as separate topics, they work hand in hand. Every knowledge area will be influenced by an item in one or more of the process groups, and vice versa.

The Baseline

In the simplest of terms, the baseline is the plan. The plan is what all elements of the project are compared to during execution of the project to ensure that the project meets specifications. It is a means to determine how performance deviates from the plan.

It is important to note that as the project progresses, the specifications may change and approved changes may alter the final output. These approved changes must be integrated into the original plan and now become the new baseline.

The cake project, for example, called for a white cake with white icing, large enough to serve 15 people and decorated with a circus theme, to be delivered on Sunday. This is the baseline for the project output.

Now, if the customer calls in and changes the order to chocolate frosting with a raspberry filling, and the design to a football theme deliverable on Saturday, this becomes our new baseline for this project. It is still a cake, serves 15, and will be iced and decorated, but changes have been approved that result in a new baseline.

Enterprise Environmental Factors

Enterprise environmental factors are factors that may influence a project's success either in a positive or negative manner. They are usually considered as inputs and may come from within the enterprise (business) or may be external inputs. These environmental inputs may include, for example:

- Government or industry regulations and standards. Local, state or federal laws and regulations may play a significant role in the progress of the project and may add prohibitive costs.
- Marketplace conditions. Marketplace conditions may indicate that the project is not needed or will not be profitable. Conversely, they may make the project one that must be undertaken to gain an advantage.
- Political climate. The political climate in the U.S. is reasonably stable; however, if a project offshore is undertaken, it is imperative to know if the government is going to be there when the project is finished.
- Stakeholder risk tolerances. Stakeholders may balk at risky projects if they are conservative as a group. A more risk-tolerant set of Stakeholders will usually be more amenable to more risk.
- Organizational culture, work ethic or culture. It is important to understand these in light of project process and acceptance.
- Human resources (HR), including a wealth or dearth of skills or knowledge. This determines how much in-house resources are available and qualified. Needing to hire outside expertise becomes expensive and may derail the project.
- Personnel issues such as staffing, training, overtime policies, etc. As with human resources, not having enough personnel to perform daily work would force the project to hire outside help.
- Commercial and company-owned technological tools. If the company has great data analytic sources, this is good for the company and the project. It is imperative to have accurate information as the project is formed.

This listing is not intended to be comprehensive; it is provided as a sampling of different situations and products that may be involved in the outcome and the success (or failure) of the project. They can influence the environment of the project, for better or worse.

Government regulations play a large part in the process of baking cakes for a bakery since they set safety standards for making the product. They are not such a big factor in a cake making project at home.

Organizational Process Assets

Organizational process assets are those that any or all of the organizations involved in the project can use to influence the project's success. These assets may include such items as plans, work templates, schedules, and organizational policies and procedures, as well as specific knowledge the company has obtained. Also included can be software and hardware that are necessary or helpful to complete the project such as financial planning, work process flow and quality control software packages.

Anything that the organization, or a contractor may use, in the course of the project work to ensure that the project is completed on time and within the scope can be considered an organizational asset. The items we talk about here are certainly only a sampling and each organization and project will include many of these and certainly will have other assets that are unique to the company or project.

Grandma is most likely the most important organizational asset in our cake project. She could be considered a wealth of information and a knowledge base for many project knowledge areas. Our 8-year-old is probably not such a valuable project asset, unless it is in the "licking the mixing spoon" phase of the project.

The History of Project Management

Project Management as a specific, defined occupation or discipline is a fairly new phenomenon but Project Management has been around for a long time. The evidence is all around us that Project Management has been a part of the human experience.

Part of the evidence is physical and can be touched, such as the Great Pyramid(s) in Egypt circa 2500 B.C., or the Inca and Aztec pyramids half way around the world in Central and South America (2000 B.C.).

The great Catholic churches that were constructed between 1000 and 1500 A.D. in Europe are shining examples of Project Management. These buildings come with a written and verbal history of how the construction process was undertaken and finally completed.

The Vikings and the English have a history of Project Management in regards to ship building and continual refinements and improvements that stretch from at least 1000 B.C. to the present day.

In the new world, examples of Project Management include Eli

Whitney, who in 1798 invented a way to make muskets with interchangeable parts. Henry Gantt gave us a structured and trackable manner in which to schedule and track productivity and stages of project progress. From WWI to the present, projects have accelerated and produced some incredible products in a very short time span. A few examples are radar, computers, including eventually personal computers, the internet, jet air travel, and nuclear energy to name a few. Also, during this time there have been many who have started to consolidate and define project and process management, including Winston Churchill.

In 1969, the Project Management Institute® was formed and project management principles and methods were codified and published.

The Future of Project Management

The future of Project Management appears to be very promising. Businesses in general are always on the lookout for cost savings and Project Management can deliver.

The need for businesses to do things faster, better and cheaper drives business leaders to find methods to accomplish these goals. In this rapidly changing global market, emerging technologies such as digitization and privatization, occurring across time zones provide opportunity for success for some businesses, and the opportunity to participate in "creative destruction" for others.

Project Managers (PMs) are in a unique position to offer expertise to those businesses that have an eye on moving forward and maintaining sector leadership and profitability.

Project Management can and most likely will be an integral part of the changing culture of the business world. The business world is evolving into a lean and agile environment, moving to dynamic processes and effectiveness and away from linear processes and efficiencies, leveraging information rather than managing it. Businesses are moving from large monolithic centrally controlled processes to smaller, nimble, autonomous project-based units and as such, Project Managers are uniquely qualified to play a major part in this "business revolution."

Project Managers can play such a role because they have multi-disciplinary and cross-disciplinary skills. They understand the basics of projects and how to move things along in a timely and efficient manner. They also understand the social and cultural interactions in the company and can work inside and outside the corporate culture to obtain results. Project Managers facilitate work processes, and provide guidance and leadership to the project teams. They keep the project organized, on track and within the scope. To do this they must create an environment that fosters involvement, commitment and collaboration, and practices conflict resolution within the company and the project teams. They possess broad skills and a deep understanding of the business and the project, which adds to their value.

As businesses move forward, leaner, more agile and more results-oriented in a globally competitive marketplace, Project Management and Project Managers stand to play an increasingly important role in this movement.

2 STARTING A PROJECT

Starting a project right is critical to its eventual success. There are many items and duties that must be identified, discussed and agreed upon before the actual "work" starts. Projects start with a great deal of discussion, discovery and planning. That is, if they are expected to produce results that satisfy the Sponsors and customers.

Develop the Project Charter

The project charter is the most important output that the project produces. Without the project charter, there is no project. The charter is essentially a contract that allows the project to be created, identifies the business need and Stakeholders, and extends the company's authorization to proceed. The charter is created during the Initiating Process Group discussions and research, and is the primary output or result of the initiating phase.

The project charter is a high-level document that outlines the project in broad terms and allows the details to be discussed and finalized in later processes.

The project Sponsor is responsible for providing the business case for the charter and the discussions framing the charter, which should outline the general requirements or objectives of the project (what the end product should look like), set boundaries and a general budget, and authorize a Project Manager.

The objectives should be SMART objectives - Specific, Measurable, Achievable, Realistic and Time Constrained. These objectives should be broad and relatively vague in the sense that this document is not the document that contains the details of the actual production work.

The charter also takes into consideration constraints that the Sponsor places on the project, such as time, budget, project boundaries, limitations and expectations for the product. Also considered will be assumptions that the Project Manager should voice, including access to subject matter experts in a timely manner, availability of materials and intellectual property, and the funds to proceed.

The charter also should mention milestones. Milestones are "markers" that are used to measure the progress of the project. These may include items such as the start date, team selection, prototype due date, etc. Milestones help keep the project focused.

A project charter for making a birthday cake may include the description of the project, making a birthday cake, the reason why a cake is being made, the type of cake and budget set aside for the cake, the criteria for delivering a satisfactory product, and the due date. If you do not have a charter, you may end up with a wedding cake a week later than you expected it at a cost that is MUCH higher than was budgeted for.

Identify the Stakeholders

Who benefits or will be harmed by this project? This is the reason to identify Stakeholders. Stakeholders are formally identified as "Persons or organizations who are actively involved in the project or whose interests may be positively or negatively affected by the performance or completion of the project."

Stakeholders are the individuals who have "skin in the game" so to speak. These individuals may include contractors, the Project Manager, subject matter experts, competitors and functional managers, as well as the project employees and customers, to name a few. There may be many or just a few, depending on the type and scale of the project.

A Stakeholder register should be created and include all Stakeholders and their roles, departments, interests, knowledge level, expectations and influence levels. It is important to know these qualities because you want to approach the correct individual or group when you need specific guidance during a task or project.

Imagine asking a baker for the money needed for cake supplies instead of the finance person. One wouldn't suppose that they would be too inclined to come up with the money. More likely they would direct you to the customer, or Sponsor for the supply money. This is the reason these traits and roles should be identified. The potential impact or support for the project that each Stakeholder brings to the project is important to determine. This Stakeholder impact recognition process allows the Project Manager (PM) to classify each Stakeholder according to their strengths and allows the PM to develop responsibilities and communication channels based upon these strengths and the potential impact to the project.

The PM should assess how the Stakeholders are going to respond to different situations, both positive and negative, as the project progresses. It is helpful to know if there is a Stakeholder who is a "hothead," who likely would create derision at every turn. In such cases, alternate communication plans would be well worth the time.

3 PLANNING A PROJECT

Planning the project is the largest process group. It entails the most processes that must be thought through, organized, planned and brought together in a cohesive and understandable structure. Planning touches every single process area and includes 20 processes. Although the planning process includes the most processes, it does not entail the most work. That is usually reserved for the executing processes.

Develop the Project Management Plan

Developing the Project Management Plan is part of the Project Integration Management knowledge area and is usually started when the charter and Stakeholder register have been completed and approved.

The plan document is the deliverable for this process group and knowledge base. The Project Management Plan should document all the actions necessary to define, plan, prepare, integrate and coordinate all component plans. This Project Management Plan is what integrates all aspects of the project. The Project Management Plan is not a hard and fast set of procedures and rules; instead it is a malleable document that may change as more knowledge is gained about the project and processes used to complete the tasks. This is known as progressive elaboration.

Because this document is dependent on knowledge gained and is flexible (within boundaries), the content and degree of formality will vary depending on the situation. There is a great deal of judgment used in the formulation of the Project Management Plan.

The Project Management Plan IS a formal, written piece of communication and is a SINGLE document that touches each of the nine knowledge areas that are part of the planning process, the Integration, Scope, Time, Human Resources, Quality, Cost, Communications, Risk and

Procurement processes. The process is iterative and ongoing, relying on a steady flow of information starting with the documents produced in the planning stages for each area. They tie back to the scope and charter.

This formal, approved document will outline and define how the project is managed, executed and controlled. The essential baselines that will be included are the Schedule Baseline, the Costs Baseline and the Scope Baseline. They allow the PM to compare actual progress to planned costs to determine the effectiveness of the program at a certain point. Certain other summary plans are integrated as they are needed such as the Human Resources plan, the Risk Management, Communications Management and Change Management, to name a few. In each area and especially overall, judgment is needed to determine just how much rigor and formality is needed for the project. This may vary greatly from project to project.

Does a Project Management Plan for making a birthday cake need to be as detailed and formal as for that of a Boeing 787? There are some serious doubts about the need for that kind of rigor and formality with a cake mix; however, if you applied the reverse, think about the result of the 787 product. Do you think the 787 would be well-constructed using a "pinch here and a dash there" standard of construction?

Collect Requirements

The Collecting Requirements process is exceptionally important to the project, in that the document created shows that the Project Manager understands the requirements and desires of the Stakeholders and the document captures the details of what is needed to successfully complete the project. This stage of the project is significant because of the impact it can have on the success of the project itself. The process includes requirement information, constraints and risks, performance goals, and other such criteria needed to consider the project a success.

The process of collecting the requirements defines and manages the Stakeholder or customer expectations and the requirements will become the basis for the Work Breakdown Structure (WBS).

The process of Collecting Requirements starts with two inputs: the Project Charter and the Stakeholder Register. The Project Charter provides a high-level description of the projects output, or product. Because this is a high-level description, it is useful in teasing out the lower level details of the project that will eventually become the work packages. The Stakeholder Register is the document that lists all project Stakeholders and their area of influence and concerns. This document will allow for quick and accurate identification of invested individuals at each stage of the project.

There are four basic steps in collecting requirements. Elicitation is the first. It is simply identifying the source(s) of the requirements and collecting the information, constraints, risks, performance goals and criteria that determine success. Requirements need to be elicited or requested (from the Stakeholders), analyzed and recorded in detail. Enough detail needs to be provided that the requirements can be measured once the project begins. These requirements now become the foundation for the Work Breakdown Schedule. The second is Analysis, which entails analyzing the concept and project requirements in light of the customer's environment, and transferring these abstract ideas and notions into a tangible, concrete form. Specification comes next. It allows the Stakeholders to review the project in its "draft" stage and to suggest, request or demand modifications to the draft, to set agreement and to get approval from the other concerned Stakeholders and the Project Manager (PM).

With the Stakeholder's help, the project details and end product vision are quantified and formally accepted. The methods used in this specification exercise may include one-on-one interviews with subject matter experts, business analysts or others. Focus groups and facilitated workshops are additional tools that use larger groups and include Stakeholders (focus) and key Stakeholders (facilitated) in groups to discuss the project needs and to elaborate requirements. These groups may use different techniques to flesh out the project requirements such as brainstorming, mind mapping, prototyping, Nominal Group, Delphi and more to produce viable project requirements and options. Decision making may be in the form of unanimity, majority, plurality or dictatorship. Each is viable and appropriate, as the situation requires or the project Sponsor supports.

This collections process is not a "one and done" process, rather it is a progressively elaborated process. That is, as more and more information comes online, it will affect the project and may need to be included in the collections process and eventually the work packets. During the entire process, a great deal of expert judgment should be sought out and included. Throughout, monitoring and controlling should be a factor.

When making a birthday cake, it is important to gather the expectations and desires of the "Cakeholders" to ensure that the Project Manager has a clear understanding that the project is a birthday cake, not a wedding cake, thus ensuring their satisfaction with the finished product. The Project Manager will then further define the project through "Cakeholder" communication, such as a face-to-face, a questionnaire, a group meeting and so on, in order to determine details of expectations for the finished product. The PM will formulate a Work Breakdown Structure (WBS) that allows budgeting and final expectations to be solidified into a plan and production to start. Remember, "Cakeholder" satisfaction is the primary consideration, always.

Define Scope

The scope is tantamount to having lines on the freeway. The white line and the rumble strip keep us from going into the ditch and the yellow center line and bots dots alert us that we are in danger of a head-on collision. Both would be potentially catastrophic mistakes that would delay the progress, cost more money and could derail the trip entirely. They are there to ensure focus on the journey and that we get to our destination safely. The scope document is much the same in that it outlines and defines the project, warns of straying off course and helps us get to the finished product with minimal delay and costs.

The scope defines clearly the requirements of the project. It is a document that explains the requirements of execution, verification, acceptance and delivery of the finished product. It must be understood by all parties that they are part of the process and must be sufficiently detailed.

When the Collect Requirements stage is completed, or nearly so, the scope document may be started. The requirements are the basis for the scope. The PM also should have the Project Charter available, as this is the guiding principle of the entire project. The PM will review the charter, requirements and any changes or modifications, and begin developing the scope.

There are many tools that may be used in developing the scope, including expert judgment from in-house or outside sources. Organizational Process Assets also should be reviewed and used if they can provide additional value in the scoping process. Why reinvent the wheel? These assets may be in the form of templates, previous projects that are similar, lessons learned on various projects or expert judgment.

Alternative Identification also should be used because this may bring into the process new or novel ideas or options that may improve the output. Facilitated workshops also may be used to bring cross-department expertise into the discussion. This type of discussion can be extremely useful in developing the scope and clarifying the understanding of the project as a whole.

The Project Scope Statement is created to level-set amongst the Stakeholders. This level-set means there is a concrete and common understanding of the scope amongst all of the Stakeholders at this juncture. The document should describe in detail the project's deliverables and the amount and type of work that is going to be necessary to create the deliverables.

The scope also allows the project team to plan the more granular aspects of the project by including the scope description, product acceptance, process and criteria, project deliverables, constraints, assumptions, and exclusions.

The scope documents should detail what IS going to be done, but just as importantly; what is NOT going to be done.

A scope document for the cake project would include, after speaking with the "Cakeholders," a description of the deliverable, in as much detail as possible. It also would describe the work process that is needed to create and finish the cake to agreed upon specifications on time. For a birthday cake baking and decorating project, there may not be a great need for a scope document, but then again, you could end up with mini cupcakes instead. Where would all the candles go?

Create a Work Breakdown Structure

The Work Breakdown Structure (WBS) is defined as: "A deliverable-oriented hierarchical decomposition of blah blah blah..." Pretty dry, but the main point is that this is THE plan for producing the goods. This is the road map!

The Work Breakdown Structure, when completed, becomes the hub of information for the project work and is exceptionally important. The WBS inputs include the Project Scope statement, requirements documentation and organizational process assets. These documents provide the details of the project work, and needs, and tie each requirement to a business need or benefit. With this information, the project can be decomposed, or broken down, into smaller and smaller tasks, or work packages.

The important concept to realize with the WBS is that this process is breaking down the product, the deliverable, into bite-size chunks of activities, not necessarily breaking the work or labor down. True, there is work that needs to be performed, however, the PM is starting with a finished product and decomposing the finished product into deliverable pieces that, once finished and assembled, become the product. Think of this as kind of reverse-engineering the product.

The WBS should be diagrammed as a hierarchical structure with the top level as the project and subsequent levels as smaller and smaller work packages to be performed to accomplish the project.

During decomposition, the goal is to create work packages that can be accomplished by an individual or a small team, in a reasonable amount of time. Reasonable is dependent on the project and may vary from half a day to a week for instance.

If it is any longer than that, it should be reviewed for further decomposition. The lowest level work packages should roll up into the next level, until they can all be consolidated into a complete project.

Decomposition should be performed until the work packages attain four attributes, and then they should be considered complete.

The four attributes are:
1. If it cannot be easily decomposed any further.
2. If it is small enough to be estimated for time or effort.
3. It is small enough to be cost estimated.
4. It may be assigned to a single person (or small group).

If the work package is contracted to an outside source, the contract work is considered a work package and the contractor will be responsible for determining the attributes.

The WBS is an exhaustive exercise that produces a graphical, hierarchical chart that is logically organized from top to bottom. Each node or level is uniquely numbered. The numbers are used to locate and identify the nodes and their associated work package assignments.

Each level of the chart is mutually exclusive and cumulatively exhaustive, meaning that there are no overlaps or gaps in the work packages and the scope is completely included with no omissions and no duplications.

One node of a WBS for making a cake may include:

1.0 Ingredients – combine and mix ingredients thoroughly.

1.1 Wet ingredients

Gather wet ingredients.

Measure and combine wet ingredients.

Mix wet ingredients thoroughly.

1.2 Dry ingredients

Gather dry ingredients.

Measure and combine dry ingredients.

Mix dry ingredients thoroughly.

As shown in this cake example, the lowest level can be accomplished by one individual and can be estimated for time and cost. The two work packages roll up into the higher level to complete the higher level node.

A WBS Dictionary is also part of the WBS exercise. This dictionary is the reference document and source of detailed information about each section of the WBS content. With the hierarchical, graphical structure of the WBS, there are limitations on how much detail and instruction can be included in each node. This document will provide additional details about the work to be completed, requirements applicable, the time and cost parameters, and account information for each node.

The WBS and the WBS dictionary now become part of the scope baseline which represents the baseline, or measuring tool for determining completion aspects of the project and is placed under control, meaning that changes to the scope must be made according to the scope management plan. Additionally, any changes to the project that occur during the WBS process should be appropriately documented in the scope and requirements documentation as part of the change management and the control and monitor process.

Define Activities

Define Activities is what it sounds like. It defines the activities that must take place in order to accomplish the work and complete the project. No magic. No mystery. Just thinking and planning.

With the birthday cake example, there is an agreed upon description of the cake, you have gathered all the ingredients, and you know when it needs to be finished and delivered. If you don't define the activities for this project you will undoubtedly miss a step. Missing the baking process may be problematic.

There are steps involved that will ensure success in the work packet and project. Defining Activities is the act of determining and recording what steps need to be taken to produce and complete an acceptable product, to complete the work packet and to eventually complete the project.

Defining Activities can be performed after the scope has been baselined (defined, agreed to and accepted). All the necessary information should be available at this juncture.

Defining Activities also is an integral part in producing the schedule so it is important to ensure it is complete and correct; however Defining Activities is NOT scheduling. It is simply identifying the various and numerous activities that are included in the project process, on a granular level.

Defining Activities is an exercise in further decomposition. It is decomposing the WBS into smaller sections called scheduling activities, which may and should be formulated with (heavy) input from the individuals directly involved, including the project teams, functional managers and possibly subject matter experts, to name a few.

When decomposition of a deliverable or sub project cannot be decomposed, or is put off for decomposition, it is called rolling wave planning. Basically, it is shifting the decomposition of less important or less time-sensitive work packets and activities until later, concentrating on the most important and timely ones now.

Tools used in this decomposition process include expert judgment, and quite a lot of it.

This helps to determine how much time and effort should be expected for each schedule activity, given the resources, physical (tools, equipment) and human. Templates and schematics from past projects, either internal or external, also should be considered. These resources provide a starting point and skeleton that can save time and energy.

The outputs from this exercise are the Activity List, Activity Attributes Document and the Milestones Document. The Activity List outlines and defines the individual activities that must be completed to consider the work packet complete. As work packets are complete they are rolled up into deliverables and finally finished.

It is important to note that the WBS and Activity List are separate entities and have different emphases. The WBS rolls up into a deliverable, whereas the activity list completes the WBS. Also, the Activity List is more closely related to the project schedule (timing) and the WBS is more closely related to the Scope Baseline.

The Activity Attributes Document is a listing of the attributes, the parts, the personnel needed, the locations the work is performed in, etc. These attributes and more, if determined needed, describe in more granular detail attributes for each activity. They extend the description of the activity and include leads or lags, constraints and assumptions, dependencies, and even required resources.

Milestones are also created during this process. Milestones are simply pre-determined "markers" in the activity, WBS, and even the project that indicate whether the work is meeting "percentage finished" and on-time for deadline goals. It is a marker that is communicated to the Stakeholders indicating progress made and is usually signed off indicating completion of a certain activity or work packet.

Sequence Activities

The Activities List is the most important document in this process and without it, there can be no sequencing. Sequencing activities is simply determining which activities need to be started and completed (or not) before the next activity can begin. Sequencing creates a logical pictorial diagram of the order of activities and their precedence relationships.

At a glance, it should be possible to tell which steps follow each other. The network paths of the activities in each project are displayed with their lead and lag times, if any, and their relationship to the previous and following activities provide for a quick and efficient visual representation of the activities order in the work packet.

To start the process, dependencies must be recognized. There are three types of dependencies:

Discretionary or soft logic. These activities, although tied to a preceding activity, may be started before the preceding activity is finished.

Mandatory or hard logic. These are mandatory activities and MUST wait until the preceding activity is finished. You MUST turn the oven on BEFORE you bake the cake.

External. These dependencies are not in the Project Manager's control and come from outside the project, including items like permitting or licensing that come from governmental agencies.

After the dependencies are identified, lags and leads are applied to the activities. Lags and leads are determinations that indicate if and when an activity may be started before the preceding activity is completed or if it must wait until after it is completed.

Using templates or a format or section of a previous project's template (sub or fragment network) from another project is a good tool to arrange the activities and work packets. Now that all of the information and a starting template have been gathered and the dependencies, leads and lags have been vetted, the Project Schedule Network Diagrams can be created. These diagrams are simply visual representations of the work sequence that need to be completed. These may be detailed to the activity level or may be higher level containing only the work packet or even the summary node levels. They will all have a starting point, end point and work process flow in between.

This is not the schedule at this point. There are no dates, times or anything else that would indicate a schedule, rather it is simply a workflow diagram.

Estimate Activity Resources

Educated guessing is just that, guessing. Some may think that estimating processes is educated guessing and to an extent, they are. These "guesses" are bolstered by hard number data, previous knowledge, estimating programs and knowledge or previous lessons learned. These resources can transform your educated guess into a result that, while it may be still somewhat vague, is narrow enough to be a reasonably accurate basis for constructing a timeline, a resource and labor schedule, and a cost estimate that can be reviewed and agreed upon by the Stakeholders, at least initially.

Estimating Activity Resources is the step in which the PM determines the effort needed to perform the activity and the number of resources that will need to be applied to the activity as well as the resource availability.

It is important to recognize how important these items are as they will eventually be used to plan the project and the schedule in the following steps.

The inputs needed are:

The Activity List. This is a listing of the activities that are included in the work package.

The Activity Attributes. An activity attributes listing complements the activity list and could be considered inseparable from the list. The attributes list gives expanded definition and information on each activity that could be useful in estimating resources needed.

Resource Calendars. These calendars determine when resources (human and physical) will be available for working on the activity. These are important to know so that the PM can orchestrate having workers and supplies together at the appropriate times.

Enterprise Environmental Factors. These are a listing of factors that may affect production, such as not having the appropriate work space or proper equipment available for an activity. If you find that you are ready to bake your cake and the facility does not have a working oven, this is an environmental factor that needs to be addressed.

Organizational Process Assets. Documents, templates, lessons learned, HR policies, staffing policies and more are considered Organizational Process Assets and need to be given consideration in the estimating process. There may be time or step-saving processes found, or there may be internal or external guidelines, policies or regulations that affect the estimation.

Expert judgment is one of the tools that will be used and most likely relied upon heavily to estimate the activity resources needed. Individuals who have performed the activity before or even whose job encompasses the activity are invaluable sources of information to estimate resources because they bring familiarity and "hands-on" experience.

Alternatives Analysis is another tool that will most likely be used in the estimating process. This involves seeking out alternatives that may save time and/or money or may increase the quality without affecting the schedule. The team may find that alternatives such as outsourcing part or all of the activity would be the best approach. Introducing software or using a different production approach are also useful alternatives in many instances.

Using published estimating data may increase the accuracy of the estimating process and may also cut down the time needed to make proper evaluations and estimates. Since there are myriad sources of published time and resource estimate data available covering a large number of activities in many industries, it is worth investigating and will help the PM gain insight into the process.

Bottom up estimating is the process of estimating each activity as it is decomposed into pieces that are small enough to quantify labor and resources needed. These estimates are then rolled up into higher level estimates for the work packages. This can be a time-consuming process; however it is usually very accurate.

Project Management software can be used to store, organize and manage all of this information obtained. The software also may be used for alternatives analysis and is a good tool for exploring alternatives.

Guidelines for effective estimating include the use of the "Golden Rules," which dictate using the right people in the process. The estimates should be based on experience. If there is not enough experience on hand, contract it or hire it. Don't negotiate the estimate, negotiate the balance (scope, schedule and cost).

Some pitfalls to avoid include giving "elevator estimates" or ambiguous expectations. Be as clear and concise with the estimates as possible. Accuracy and honesty up front is essential for creating a good working relationship and trust with the Stakeholders.

Also, be aware this is an estimate of activity resources; this is not a bid for the job. These two things are very different. The bid *includes* the activity estimates, whereas the estimates are *part of*, the bid. Lastly, avoid the temptation to pad the estimate with extra resources, either human or physical. It is better to give an accurate representation; be clear, honest and transparent to the Stakeholder. Contingency plans can be created if there are any anticipated difficulties.

The outputs from this exercise are the Activity Resource Requirements, the Resource Breakdown Structure and the Project Documentation Updates.

The Activity Resource Requirements document needs to specify in a detailed manner what resources are needed for each activity. This information should include the type and number of resources needed. It should detail for instance if five journeymen bakers are needed or one journeyman and one apprentice are needed to bake the birthday cake.

The Resource Breakdown Structure is a document that is similar to the WBS in that it is a hierarchal and graphical, allowing the PM or anyone else involved in the project the activity resources needed for which activities and when they are needed. It should be logically arranged from top to bottom and then by category and type of resources.

Project Documents Updates that occur during the process are documented and then communicated to the PM and Control and Monitor area. The activity and attributes lists should be updated. The calendar also may be updated at this time if there are resources that need to be reserved or activities that need to be considered before starting.

Estimate Activity Durations

Are we there yet? Most every parent has heard this question and most every kid remembers saying it, at least once. Estimate Activity Durations are one of the keys to answering this question before the Stakeholder asks. It is also a process that is exactly what it sounds like, applying a time measurement to an activity. The measurement may be minutes, hours, days or weeks, and maybe more, but the important thing to realize is that every activity should have a time standard.

The duration is a measurement of time and not an indicator of the level of effort or resources needed to complete the activity, although these need to be considered when assigning a time to an activity.

Considering the baking time of a birthday cake is approximately one hour and you have a project calling for 10 cakes, could you bake all of them in one hour? Could you and nine other bakers each bake a cake in 10 separate ovens in one hour? The duration estimate will be affected by the resources available; however the resources should not necessarily determine the time duration.

Having and assigning these time measurements allows the PM to use this document as a primary input into the creation of the work schedule when the overall project timeline is being created.

The primary inputs for this process are the:

Activity Lists. Every activity in the list should receive a time duration assessment to determine the appropriate amount of time the activity will be assigned.

Activity Attributes, nearly inseparable from the activity list, describe in greater detail the tasks in the activity list.

Activity Resource Requirements. These resource requirements may determine how expeditiously the activity is completed.

Resource Calendars allow the PM to see which resources, both human and physical, are available at what times. This is necessary to know when making the schedule.

Project Scope Statement. This contains information about constraints and assumptions that were made about the project that may affect the activity. Examples of constraints and assumptions would include off-site construction, outsourcing design, if the production is time-constrained, etc.

Enterprise Environmental Factors. Regulations, company policy, safety standards, documentation requirements, and other corporate and governmental requirements may affect the duration of the activity. If an activity must be safety documented at each step, or a government sign-off is required at certain phases, they must certainly be considered when allocating time.

Organizational Process Assets. These assets may be historical information, templates, notes from previous similar projects, or any such documentation that could provide data and information valuable to estimating the time duration of the activities.

Expert judgment is an invaluable tool in estimating the duration of an activity and a project. Time is notoriously hard to estimate and those with expert judgment should have some background or familiarity with the project and process, and should follow some basis, such as historical information and experiences, or statistical.

Analogous or top down estimating is used when there are similar projects performed in the same company. The time to complete the first activity with a healthy dose of expert judgment is used as a basis for setting duration for a similar activity.

Parametric estimating uses known time estimate quantities to estimate the activity duration. An example of parametric estimating, as discussed earlier, can be illustrated with the cake baking duration. If a cake takes one baker one hour, then we can use parametric estimating to conclude that a team of 10 bakers can bake 10 cakes in one hour.

Three Point Estimating. Three point estimating is taking an average of three deliberate estimates. The first is a most likely scenario (M), the second is a pessimistic scenario (P) and the third is an optimistic (O) scenario. The three-point estimate adds the three values and divides by three to obtain an average. A variation of the three-point is the PERT estimate which is nearly identical to the 3-point except that the most likely (M) is weighted. The formula now reflects the weight and appears; (P + (4*M) + O)/6.

After these estimates are performed, there may be a reserve estimate calculated and set aside as a contingency in case the project incurs slippage. This is to identify the possibility of a contingency situation and not intended to pad the estimate.

The outputs for this process include the Activity Duration Estimates, which outline the duration estimates of all activities in the project. The estimates should represent a range instead of a single static number for each activity. Project Documentation Updates also are produced and changes to the activity attributes, a normal part of this process, must be updated. Also, any changes to the assumptions or constraints should be documented.

Develop Schedule

The Develop Schedule process could be viewed as the Estimate Project Duration exercise. The process of developing a schedule is one of the most important parts of the project simply because it will be used by virtually everyone involved in the project. It is a highly visible time management document that is intended to keep the project on track concerning attaining start and finish times, and to achieve project completion intermediate milestones.

This process is one of the largest of the processes and makes use of 21 combined tools, inputs and outputs.

Developing the schedule usually takes place after the activities have been defined and sequenced and the activity resources and durations have been estimated. The schedule is usually an iterative process allowing for changing resources or activity sequences. This document results in the Schedule Baseline which, when finished and approved, is the document that will be used to track the project performance against.

The inputs used in the schedule process are the same as those used in the previous process and include the activity list/attributes, project schedule network diagrams, activity resource requirements, resource calendars, activity duration estimates, the project scope statement enterprise environmental factors and organizational process assets. There is one new input mentioned, the activity duration estimate, which is the output from the last process.

Generally, the tool used for developing the schedule is the Schedule Network Analysis and is actually a group of techniques used in the process.

Critical Path method is one such technique. The critical path defines the path of activities that, if any are delayed, will delay the entire project. There are three main purposes to finding the critical path. The first is to determine the project's finish date. The second is to identify how much float each activity in the paths have.

How much can an activity be delayed without upsetting the project deadline? Finally, identify those activities with the highest risk, those that cannot slip without making the entire project late. The Critical Path is the path that takes the longest to complete and therefore has no flex in the timeline. It would throw the entire project into failure by not hitting the target or completion date.

Three questions or calculations that are involved in determining Critical Path are the Forward Pass, the Backward Pass and the calculation of float.

The Forward Pass is working through the activities from the start date and determining dependencies to estimate when the activities will be expected to start. For example, if we start activity A on week one and it takes two weeks to complete, then activity B will start on the first day of week three. Work moving forward through the activities to determine start and completion dates.

The Backward Pass is working backward from the target finish date and determining how much float or delay can be tolerated without moving the target date. It is determining the latest start date possible. This can be achieved by adding the float in the project to the early start date as determined in the previous calculation.

Calculating float, or the amount of time that an activity has before a mandatory start date, can be a valuable tool in evaluating the critical path and the related paths of related activities in the work packet, determining the completion date and even reassigning resources or activities should the need arise.

The Critical Chain method is nearly identical to the Critical Path method except that with the critical chain method, the activities are analyzed as aggressively as possible and a buffer is set aside for use in managing slippage anywhere in the chain. Management is usually aware of the buffer; however it is not usually told to the workers.

Resource leveling is used in scheduling after the critical path is determined. Resource leveling is assigning resources to activities to determine what will happen to the project schedule. This tool allows the PM to see what will happen if there are not enough resources to complete the activity as first estimated. The activity and the path will be re-evaluated and the schedule will be leveled to account for resources.

What-if scenario is another tool used and often it is employed using a Monte Carlo analysis. This analysis systematically applies myriad variables to the activities and processes to obtain the best scenario for scheduling results. Leads and lags also must be applied to the process and activities as part of the scheduling process as they become apparent, usually after the Monte Carlo analysis, and are used to tighten up and optimize the schedule. Schedule compression may also be considered at this point in the process and involves reviewing the schedule and activities to determine if crashing or fast tracking are appropriate.

Crashing is a term used to describe accelerating an activity, shortening its duration, by "crashing the resources," or adding more people.

Fast tracking is simply the process of overlapping activities that may be started at the same time or close in start times that will not adversely affect each other. For instance, when baking a cake, one person may mix the dry ingredients and another the wet ingredients at the same time with no adverse affect on the project.

It would create a problem though if you tried to fast track the baking and icing process. The cake must completely bake and cool before the icing is applied; this is non-negotiable.

A scheduling tool can be an invaluable tool because it facilitates the math and logic processes that are part of the process. There are many different tools on the market that have many different price points and capability levels.

The outputs for this process are the Project schedule. The schedule should include every activity and the start, finish and durations, as well as dependencies. The schedule also should contain the project start and finish dates. Typically the schedule will be in a graphical format such as a Project Network Diagram or a Gantt (bar) chart.

The network diagram is a detail driven tool that arranges activities in their designated paths displaying dependencies and sequencing. It is useful to determine critical path, as well as lead and lag times.

Gantt charts are graphical charts that represent the activities as a bar that stretches over a time period. Each activity in a project has a separate bar. It is easy to see a high-level view of start and end dates and if there is

Douglas C. Ruh Jr.

overlap in activities. This chart does contain the activity information; however it is best used as an overview or a management and Stakeholder reporting tool.

Milestone charts may and should be developed at this time as well. Milestone charts contain information on significant milestone events or project deliverables in each activity. These are high-level charts that are useful in reporting progress against the schedule, to management and to Stakeholders.

The schedule baseline is created and approved by the Stakeholders and the Sponsor at this point. The schedule data is compiled. This is data that supports and explains the decision making that went into the schedule process. It is a document that could be useful for upcoming projects.

The project document updates further outline the reasons decisions were made and adjustments that were applied to the schedule during the process.

Estimate Costs

Have you allocated enough money for the project to see it to completion or will funding dry up halfway through the process? How do you even know? This is the basis for the Estimate Costs process. This process involves estimating what the project would cost (figuratively) today. It is at a point in time and not a one-and-done process, since prices on everything change, sometimes down, mostly up, and it is nearly impossible to tell what they are going to be in a year. Since estimating costs is inclusive, and would include supplies and labor, it is important that the correct inputs are obtained, including the:

Scope Baseline. This is the original plan plus all approved changes.

Project Schedule. This schedule shows when each activity will begin and end. It also shows the planned start and finish dates of the project as a whole.

Human Resources Plan. This plan document outlines roles and responsibilities for those involved in the project. It also contains the staffing management plan and organizational charts documenting the areas, titles and levels of the participants. This is the who, what, where and when for the people participating in the project.

Risk Register. This is the document that lists the perceived risks that may affect the project, either negatively or positively. It is a continually changing document.

Enterprise Environmental Factors. Although on a definitional level there is one definition laid out, it is useful to note here that the environmental factors may change with each process area.

Organizational Process Assets that are on hand and appropriate to the process and,

Expert Judgment. This is the judgment of experienced individuals who have performed similar projects. This is a recurring theme in many of the project steps.

The WBS should provide the framework for the activities and projects that need to be considered in their entirety and then costed out to obtain the basis for the estimate.

Given that the WBS provides a detailed record of upcoming events and activities, this is a great tool to employ for performing a "bottom up" estimation. This is estimated by taking each of the lowest level activities, applying costing to them to obtain a cost for each activity and then simply starting to roll costs up. As the costs are aggregated at each higher level, the top level provides a reasonably accurate estimate total. This process may be overly time-consuming, though.

Another strategy which takes the opposite tack is the summary or "top down" strategy, where management estimates the project, usually at the beginning of the process as a mechanism to plan their yearly budget. This process is a high-level, informal and inaccurate process that is used as a placeholder in the budget.

In addition to estimating the direct costs there are two concepts that should be considered in the process. They are Life Cycle Costing and Value Engineering. Life Cycle Costing is the practice of considering the cost of ownership of the product including creation, operating, and eventually the replacement and disposal of the product.

This concept forces the big picture view, not just the "I need it now" view of the product.

Value Engineering speaks more to the project and activities because it is trying to engineer value into the process. Value is generally considered to be increasing the bottom line, decreasing time to completion and other costs, and generally squeezing every bit of value from a project. It is important to realize that these concepts and the estimating process itself are ongoing processes and should be reviewed regularly throughout the project because things are constantly changing. Change may come in the form of higher materials costs, labor cost increases or availability decreases, etc. In any style that is used, direct costs, and costs that are incurred because the project is undertaken as well as indirect costs and contingency reserves are taken into account and factored into the estimate. Indirect costs are incurred regardless of whether the project was undertaken; however the project will use some of these resources because they are on hand and will be allocated. Contingency reserves are set aside to cushion the effect of slippage in the project process or budget.

There are tools that are used in the process that help the PM in the estimating process. These tools include Analogous Estimating, which is a fancy term that means "we did this before so we should use the estimate again." Well, maybe not exactly that but it is a reasonable analogy. Analogous estimations are using the estimates from similar projects that have been completed by the company previously. They are easy to use because the framework and many of the rates and times are already in place. The drawback is noted if the project is not the same or was complete quite a while in the past, wherein the time and materials data may be stale and the estimate therefore, inaccurate.

If we baked a scratch chocolate cake last week that serves five people, and it cost $10 in materials and was completed by two bakers in three hours, it would be safe to assume that if the current project is a vanilla scratch cake serving five, the analogous estimate would be appropriate. Would it still be appropriate if the original project was completed three years ago? How about if the original cake was a box mix?

Parametric Estimating is another tool available. This type of estimating involves known quantities, or static costs. This is a reasonable process if the project cost is known and it is a matter of scalability. To explain this in baker's terms, if you know that a cake costs $10 to make and serves five people, then you can easily calculate how much a cake would cost that would feed 25 people. Simply divide 25 people by five servings per cake and you would need the equivalent of five cakes. Five cakes times $10 is an estimated cost of $50.

Bottom up estimating is a very accurate and thorough manner of estimating. This entails costing each activity for materials and labor and incidentals, if any. Each activity is then rolled up into the work package and the work packages rolled up into the project nodes, and so on until you have rolled everything into one project estimate. This is not only highly accurate, but it is also highly time-consuming.

Three point or PERT estimating can also be performed by taking an estimate of the pessimistic (highest) cost, the most likely cost and the optimistic (lowest) costs and averaging these out. PERT estimating gives more weight to the most likely estimate and should be more accurate than the 3-point. The PERT formula is Pessimistic + 4(most likely) + Optimistic /6!

A Reserve Analysis is another tool that is used to help ensure that the project can meet the budgetary limits by creating a contingency or buffer amount in the process. The buffer can be applied to selected work packages, activities or nodes, or accumulated as an overall project contingency. This is incorporated into the planning to ensure that any work or budget slippage is covered.

Cost of quality (COQ) is a technique that is used to evaluate all of the costs associated with making the product to certain specification of quality level. Generally, the higher quality product that is demanded, the more the cost to produce. The opposite is also true and is known as the Cost of Poor Quality (COpQ) and these items are not conforming to the established quality standards. The costs can be illustrated with our cake example and buying cake flour. If our cake ingredients cost $10 for a scratch cake, this estimate includes the flour we need. The quality level will be set for a high-quality, all-purpose flour. If we increase the quality by importing an exotic low gluten Durham "00" flour mixture with chestnut flour incorporated, the cost is $9 a pound. The cost of "quality" just blew our budget. On the other hand, if we borrow flour from our neighbor, it is free!

The catch is that it has been sitting around for five years and is now rancid. Presto! The cost of poor quality is now apparent, as is the level of our shame and embarrassment. Ensuring that the cost of quality meets specifications can prevent process or product failure and/or rework.

One last tool to touch on is project estimating software that can be used to help with systematically performing the estimating. The software simply does the job instead of pencil and paper. The computer can perform the calculations and scenarios quickly and efficiently. Also, the program will be helpful in organizing and storing the project and product data that are used in building the estimate. Vendor bid analysis is used to review outside bids for the project. Winning bids should be evaluated specifically, in order to understand what the winning bid company is doing to perform the process, on time and within budget. These lessons can be applied to future projects.

The Level of Accuracy that needs to be obtained in order to consider the project a success is another factor in the estimating process and is usually based on cost sensitivity. In the outset of the process a "Rough Order of Magnitude" standard may be used since the estimate will be high level and pretty much best guess. It will essentially be a placeholder estimate to reserve funds and serve notice that the plan will cost money. This estimate is very rough and may vary within a range of -25% to 75% of the actual estimated costs.

Budget Estimating is a tighter and more concise estimate and is based on a more complete and detailed costing data and information. This estimate is accurate within a range of -10% to 25%. This estimating is usually performed by the team leads and is suitable for planning.

The Definitive Estimate is the most detailed and accounts for cost estimating down to the activity level, and even the sub-activity level if necessary. Team members are generally recruited for this level of detail and because the detail is so closely scrutinized and considered, the range of accuracy is -5% to 10%.

When considering the approach and the variables involved in the process, units of measurement need to be discussed, reviewed and agreed upon to track costs. Will the PM use hours for tracking? Using hours is pretty easy but it will force the PM into a rougher estimate of the costs. This is because although you can track each hour, labor and materials will be averaged. How about using a lump sum for each activity or work package? Lump sum tells the PM "here's what you get, make it work." What if there are increases in time, labor or supplies? Actual labor and materials usage is the most accurate but also the most time consuming. The PM will use a method that best fits the project and the Sponsor's risk tolerance. The PM also will inquire about organizational links such as a chart of accounts and an accounting system that could be used to help track activities and costs. These, when available, save the cost of buying or creating new, keep the information in-house and available, and are familiar to the functional managers. Having these accounts set up and trackable allows for easy monitoring of the Control Thresholds, limits agreed upon that are in place that trigger responses. The control thresholds provide a warning mechanism of an activity or work package that is approaching the threshold and should be considered, usually a percentage over or under from budget. This information also needs to be communicated to the right people at the right time and the right responses should be obtained if there is a threshold met. Communication should be easy to understand and have enough detail to provide a clear explanation. Whether that is a table, graphic or a written memo, the information should be available on a regular basis, as the business needs and Sponsor risk tolerances indicate.

Finally we get to outputs! There are three outputs from this exercise and they are the Activity Cost Estimates, the Basis of Estimates and the Project Document Updates.

The Activity Cost Estimates are pretty straightforward. They are the costing estimates of every activity included in the project.

The Basis of Estimates is the supporting data that went into the data costing decisions. It is important to provide enough information and detail to explain how you arrived at the cost estimates.

The Project Document Updates. Updates will invariably happen in the cost management plan discussions and they will need to be integrated into the project document.

Determine the Project Budget

Now that we know what the pieces will cost, we need to know what the project will cost and more importantly, will the Sponsor approve the costs and sign off on the cost baseline? In other words, will we have a job in the morning? Now is the time to put it all together and pin down the costs to work packages and put dates on the schedule.

After the activities, their durations and resources have been fleshed out and the schedule has been developed, it is time to determine the budget. The budget constitutes the funds that the Sponsor and company have allocated and authorized to execute the project. It is also known as the cost performance baseline. The actual cost performance, that is, if the project is on budget, over or under budget in any activity or work packet will be compared to the baseline. It is important to be explicit as possible and include any assumptions that may affect the budget. If you know that there are going to be labor contract negotiations three months after the project is started and there is likely to be a 3% raise in wages, you probably should include this assumption in the budgeting information.

There are a number of inputs that will be useful, and necessary, in the process and should be at hand and consulted regularly during the process.

The Activity Cost Estimates have the costs for every activity in the project calculated and documented. These are important for determining the budget and schedule.

The Basis of Estimates is useful to determine if the reasoning for the activity costs are sound. If they are found to be flawed, they need to be revisited.

The Scope Baseline is necessary because it includes the project scope statement, the WBS and the WBS dictionary. These are important because they help explain the scope and why it was set, and any constraints and assumptions that were included, and limits imposed.

The Project Schedule ties costs back to activities and to certain points in the timeline of a project. It helps in planning when costs will be occurring.

Resource Calendars are integral to scheduling the proper people or equipment to perform activity work. This is knowledge that is important in planning when costs are going to be incurred.

Contracts for parts of the project should provide information about how much the company is obligated to pay the contracting company and when the money is due.

Organizational Process assets that could be useful may include templates, software that may be used for planning, estimating data for budgeting and scheduling, and historical information that is relevant, to name a few.

Taking information from all of these sources, the budget can now be constructed.

Cost Aggregation is usually the primary manner in which the budget is constructed. During cost aggregation, costs are aggregated at lower levels into higher levels, up to the singular project total cost. Since all activities have been costed out, it is relatively simple to roll each activity cost up to obtain a work packet total. The work packet totals can then be aggregated to obtain a project node total, and so on. This method makes it easy to monitor, measure and control progress and costs at lower levels like the work package level. This process produces estimated timing of the costs as was determined in the scheduling process.

Reserve Analysis is determining the risk to the project before the risk happens and costs a lot of money. By performing a risk analysis, the PM and Sponsor can set a contingency reserve aside. The contingency reserve is a hedge against unforeseen or foreseen risks happening. The company is funding its own catastrophic insurance fund. The PM usually has the authority to access the funds when needed, given certain parameters.

The Sponsor and company executives may also set aside a Management Reserve that is "off the books," that is, not part of the baseline as far as the PM is concerned. This is the type of reserve the PM does not usually know about, rather the Sponsor has held this out just in case the project incurs any unplanned changes to the project scope and cost that are not covered by the contingency reserves.

Funding Limit Reconciliation is another tool used to determine the budget. This simply indicates that somewhere along the line, when management first conceived the project, they allocated budgeted funds for the project, sometimes not even knowing the scope of the project, much less the accurate cost estimate. Because the budget, the initial cost target, has been determined beforehand, this new, more detailed and accurate budget document must be reconciled to the existing and any inconsistencies and cost variances must be resolved before the costs are baselined.

Expert judgment is applied to the process to ensure that the costs, timing and budgets are accurate and reasonable.

This is usually obtained from the person performing or responsible for the activity and should be consulted for input.

Outputs from the budgeting process are the Cost Performance Baseline, or the approved budget, and the Funding Requirements. The Cost Performance Baseline specifies what costs will be incurred AND when they will be incurred in the course of the project. There may be one baseline or there may be multiple baselines. The PM may decide to keep a labor cost baseline for in-house labor and a separate one for contracted labor. Generally cost baselines form an "S" pattern on a grid chart. This is because costs usually start off slowly, build during high production times and then taper and flatten out as the activity or project winds down.

The accompanying output is the Project Funding Requirements, which allows the company to know when funds will be needed, and generally how much funding is needed at different stages of project completion.

Using the cost baseline the company can schedule funding need that is in concert with the baseline. This alleviates the necessity of submitting expense claims to management for approval and reimbursement.

The cost baseline and funding requirements allow the Sponsor and PM of our cake project to know that there will be a time when ingredients must be purchased. Because of these budgeting documents, the Sponsor can anticipate that there will be money needed at a certain time for supplies to be purchased. The baker can avoid buying eggs, submit a reimbursement form, buy flour, submit a form, etc.

Plan Quality

Quality is not an accident. Project Managers don't trip and fall into a big 'ole puddle of quality. They plan for quality. They make it part of the focus of the project and the ideal that the end product is to meet, which brings us to defining what quality is.

Quality is fulfilling the (stated or implied) requirements of the project. It is not a particular grade or category, it is simply and importantly, hitting the mark of what the project Sponsor has said is needed as the final product. This is a different definition than most of us think of quality in terms of. Usually we think of quality as GRADE.

Think about this using something everyone can relate to – FOOD. We don't usually think of fast food burgers as quality; however they are a decidedly fine example of quality. They are designed (I know, odd to think of a burger as designed) to have certain characteristics visually, for taste, and have a certain mouthfeel. That a chain can meet these requirements time after time indicates that they have designed their burger and attained their quality goals. Especially when you throw into the design that the burgers must meet a certain price point (one dollar) and time to prepare for customer delivery (under two minutes).

Let's take a look at a 100% top sirloin Kobe beef hamburger offered at a gourmet steakhouse. This burger also has been designed using particular quality standards and has met them. The burger may be hand-pressed using top grade meat, freshly baked artisan bread and top drawer condiments. Is this a higher quality burger than the fast food restaurant? In the PM world, no, it is not. It meets the same level of quality because it meets the standards that the Sponsors required. It may be of a higher GRADE, but not necessarily quality.

Let's get started planning our quality. To plan our quality we do need some guidelines and standards that will come from documents we have already created. The Scope Baseline, Stakeholder Register, Cost Performance Baseline, Schedule Baseline, Risk Register, Enterprise Environmental Factors and Organizational Process Assets are all needed and will be used to plan quality. Remember, quality is planned in, not inspected in. These documents contain the essential elements and details of the project and the product therefore are essential to *planning in quality*. The reason the PM plans in quality is that it is more effective to carry out the project build and it is cheaper.

Briefly, the PM understands these documents and the importance they hold and it is worth mentioning them again here.

The Scope Baseline lays out the project description, major project deliverables and the criteria that will be used for acceptance of the product. Included also are the WBS that identify the work packages and their deliverables. It also includes control accounts used to monitor and measure project performance. The WBS Dictionary is part of the WBS and defines WBS elements, activities and technical information needed in the project production. The Stakeholder Register is a listing of Stakeholders that may have an impact on the project. These are the people that have skin in the game. The right product at the right time at the right price matters greatly to them. The Cost Performance Baseline and Schedule Baseline are two documents that help to monitor planned costs and any cost overruns and planned scheduling and schedule overruns. These are important documents that keep the "right cost and right time" elements in check. The Risk Register identifies known risks to the project. These risks may be known or unknown but have the potential to throw the cost or schedule off track. Realize that this is usually viewed as a negative, but the risk may have a positive effect. This register is updates as needed and is in a continual state of flux. Organizational Process Assets include the company Quality Policy, which sets the intended direction of the company as far as quality is concerned. If there is no quality policy, one should be discussed and drafted for the project. Also included may be historical databases, lessons learned, documents from previous similar projects and other such data that will help the project.

To help plan the quality, there are a number of analytical tools available to the PM to use in guiding the planning process.

The Cost Benefit Analysis is a common tool that is used frequently across business applications to determine if the project will add value to the company. To illustrate this concept, if the PM is planning the quality of our cake and has a budget of $10 to create a child's birthday cake from scratch, the PM can certainly increase or decrease the grade of the product. Does the cost provide a benefit? If the cake turns out to be a $50 cake equivalent to a wedding cake, the build was too expensive for the project parameters. Delicious, but we broke the bank. What if the PM made one cupcake at a cost of $1? We have surplus money but not enough product. This is equally as bad.

The Cost of Quality is another technique that is used in Project Management. The theme here is to capture all costs used and needed to produce a product that is deliverable. It captures all costs over the life of the project needed to prevent either non-conformance to the specifications or failure of the product. The idea here is to build in enough costs for preventative measures such as training, documenting and adjusting processes, procuring the correct equipment and scheduling time, as well as for detective measures like inspecting and testing the product to cut down on failures. Get it right the first time. These are the costs of conformance (to the quality plan). Costs of nonconformance include reworking or scrapping the product or project from an internal failure viewpoint, or worse, from an external viewpoint, warranty work, liabilities, and loss of reputation and business. "If mama ain't happy, ain't nobody happy." Replace the word customer for mama.

Benchmarking and using Control Charts are additional tools the PM has available to determine and plan quality. Benchmarking utilizes data from actual or planned project practices and sets targets, or benchmarks to compare actual and planned progress against a similar project with the intent to find best practices, new ideas for production and for measuring project performance against a known set of criteria. In effect, it is taking away a lot of guesswork.

Control charts are charts that use upper and lower acceptable limits for the project (or even the work packages). These charts illuminate the project process and are a visual comparison to the actual work product compared to upper and lower control levels. The aim is to keep the actual work product measurement line as close to the middle of the upper and lower limits as possible.

Design of Experiments is a tool, a statistical method used to identify specific factors that might influence specific variables of a process or product. This technique involves experimenting with different elements of the process, especially those thought to be vulnerable, and testing different process techniques, and logging the results. This technique should reveal the best practices in production and changes can be made to enhance and bolster the process.

Statistical sampling is simply choosing a sample and inspecting the product at certain points. If a 10% sample is used, then at a certain point on an assembly line for instance, 10 out of every 100 widgets will be pulled from the line and inspected for quality. Corrections to the process and product can be made if there is a flaw found.

Finally, flowcharting the process will allow everyone involved to see and understand the process. This will work to highlight potential choke points, decision points and the order in which the process flows.

Along with these tools, there are management methodologies such as Six Sigma, Total Quality Management and others that may be used to determine and test acceptable thresholds. There are other planning tools that have already been discussed such as brainstorming, Affinity Programs,

Force Field Analysis and Nominal Group Techniques that may prove useful and fruitful in planning quality.

The outputs for this Planning Quality process include the:

Quality Management Plan, which describes how the Project Management Team will implement the quality policy. This plan is a component of, and provides input to, the project management plan and includes quality control, quality assurance and continuous process improvement approaches to the project.

Quality Metrics is another output. A metric is a very specific operational definition outlining the specific quality measurements, product and project attributes, and methods to measure quality of them. The metrics include measurements, which are specific, actual values and tolerances which are acceptable variations. One pound of flour for our cake is a specific, actual measurement. One pound of flour +/- 0.5 oz. is a tolerance threshold.

Quality Checklists are a set of structured checklists that ensure that a project's steps and requirements are completed. It's a "to-do" list.

Process Improvement Plans detail the steps that will be taken to analyze parts of the process and activities, and make improvements to enhance the process.

Project Document Updates. Any changes needed to the project documents including the Stakeholder Register or the Responsibility Assignment Matrix to name just two.

We have covered a lot of ground in this heading. The main point is to plan, plan, plan! Plan your quality in the product and project to give yourself every chance to succeed.

Develop the Human Resources Plan

Without people, you just have a pile of stuff. Developing the Human Resources (HR) Plan is a process that involves people. It involves identifying people with the skills to accomplish the activities and the project. These skills and attributes include management skills, communication skills, mechanical and technical skills, people relations skills, and more. This iterative process is needed because it allows the PM to lay out how to staff, manage, team build, and assess and improve the project team.

The inputs for the Develop Human Resources (HR) Plan include the activity resource requirements, the enterprise environmental factors and the organizational process assets. The output will be the Human Resources Plan document. So far so good, and pretty straightforward. The plan will include a timetable for acquiring the human resources needed for each activity and the duration each is needed as well as a release date. The people (resources) who will be tapped for the project will have defined roles, thus eliminating any confusion and avoiding power struggles or turf wars.

Market conditions should be addressed during the process. This is an exercise that addresses the surplus or scarcity of qualified resources available for the activities and project. If there are scarce resources, outsourcing, hiring and additional training all should be considered. Team building, legal and company policy compliance also should be discussed as these constraints, as well as others, should be addressed during the planning stage.

The tools that may be used during the HR planning process are organizational charts (org charts) and position descriptions, and may be represented in a hierarchical, matrix or text format. The visual hierarchical, "tree" format is the most common and widely understood visual chart in the business world. It is a top to bottom chart that shows the relationship between the top person at each level of management, and employees below. At a glance it is easy to determine levels of authority, reporting chain and position descriptions.

Matrix charts are popular charts that use intersecting rows and column information to outline an individual's responsibilities on an activity. A RAM chart (Responsibility Assignment Matrix) is often used and the most popular is called the RACI (**R**esponsibility, **A**ccountability, **C**onsulted, **I**nformed) chart. Each individual is listed on a row and the intersecting duties are listed in the column headers. The intersecting boxes have one of four letters R (responsible), A (accountable), C (consult), or I (inform) entered, indicating their primary assignment for that activity. Generally, one person is responsible for the work package but different people may be held responsible for the activities in the work package. The RACI chart quickly and visually displays the needed authorities.

Text formats are usually written out in a job description format and are most useful when recruiting candidates for the project. When recruiting candidates, networking within the organization provides the PM with a good understanding of the political and organizational dynamics of the organizations. They can not only find qualified candidates for the activity, they also may be able to influence the project through this knowledge.

Common roles in the HR plan include the Sponsor, Project Manager, Customer, Team Lead, Functional Manager and regulatory specialists.

The Sponsor is where the buck stops. He or she is the individual who is paying the bills, influencing the proper people to move the project, providing support and backup, and approving the project and the charter. Basically they are the high level go-to person. He or she has the authority and power to make things happen or to stop them completely.

Douglas C. Ruh Jr.

The Project Manager is the agent of action for the Sponsor. The PM has the authority to perform the project. They also are responsible for all aspects of the project, including identifying and communicating to the Stakeholders, Sponsor, customer and employees. They perform the initial and continual planning, and monitor all aspects of the project including time, HR, risks and costs.

The customer is the recipient of the final product and is included as necessary in the project to provide funding, outline requirements and changes to their requirements.

Team Lead is the person that is doing the work on the line. They are managing the teams of employees, timelines, budgets and production. They are contributing their time and skills to the project.

Functional Managers are those that have long-term control over the department. They control the use of their employees and department resources over the longer term. They have long-term control over their staff and can release the right people at the right time, affecting the project.

Regulatory specialists may be inspectors who must sign off on activities, legal specialists that may stop a project for liability, etc. These are the people who ensure that the project complies with the law and local regulations.

The HR Plan is the sole output for this process and is mainly comprised of the roles and responsibilities document, organizational charts and the staffing management plan.

The roles and responsibilities component contains the defined roles, level of responsibility, authority level, skill level and title of the role or "position" that is needed to be filled for the project.

The staffing management plan details how many people will be used, when and in which areas, and when they are released from the project.

Other components of the HR plan may consist of a histogram and would graphically show the highest and lowest human resource needs and usage. A timeline also is needed to help management anticipate and plan for the staffing that is needed at point along the project. A release plan should be part of the timeline. It is important to be able to declare a release date for the employees and return them to their functional departments.

Plan Communications

Should you be a "Great Communicator" or should you be a great firefighter? Communication is the key to ensuring that the project is completed, on time and to specifications. Without communication, the PM will not have the ability to predict activity timing, foresee problems and formulate plans to keep the project O.T.I.S. (to borrow a phrase from a concrete company) on time, in spec.

The inputs used for planning communications are the Stakeholder register, the Stakeholder management strategy, the enterprise environmental factors and the organizational process assets.

These tools are used to ensure that communication is taking place. Furthermore that the right communication is given to the right people at the right time in the right format and that only the pertinent information is presented. This is not a "blast email" format. PMs should be spending the greater part of their time communicating to project managers, Stakeholders and Sponsors.

To start, a good tool to use is a Stakeholder grid. This grid helps to assess the relative importance of the Stakeholder to the project and how much and what type of information each should receive. To accompany this, a communications plan document should be created that details the communications type for each Stakeholder. It should include areas of information, type of communication, frequency of communication, etc.

When formulating the plan it is important to note that the more Stakeholders that you have, the more channels there are going to be. For example, if you have four Stakeholders, there will be six lines of communication and if you add a fifth Stakeholder, the channels increase to 10.

It is important therefore to be aware of this complexity and create a plan that includes official lines of communication, especially with the Sponsor, contractors and outside Stakeholders.

To complicate things even further, there are many types of communication that may be utilized including informal written such as email and memos, formal written like the project charter and contracts, informal verbal such as meetings, discussions and phone calls and formal verbal, which includes speeches, mass communications and presentations.

All of these also need to be communicated by different methods that include interactive communication. This is a give-and-take style such as an email chain or a conversation. Push communications could include an email that does not require an answer or a notice on the bulletin board. Pull communications also are an option and would take the form of a blog or intranet site that invites others to access information.

Listening skills are also important to the communication plan and include active listening. Listen to the other party, engage and ask questions to ensure there is adequate and accurate understanding. The PM also needs to be aware of nonverbal cues and paralingual cues. These speak, often times, louder than the words used.

Using a well-established communications plan and engaging in good communication and listening skills will often head off problems down the road. It will allow for negotiating equitable agreements and preventing conflict. A little time and planning here go a long way to make the project run more smoothly.

Identify Risks

Aye matey, up to the crow's nest with your spyglass and scan the horizon for risk! It is out there ahead of us somewhere and we need to have fair warning.

Risk is always out there, ahead of us, in the future. It is an uncertain or even unforeseen event that if it takes place will have an impact on the project.

Risks can affect one or any number of facets of the project including the scope, schedule, the cost of labor or materials, or the quality of the finished product. When the risks are known or anticipated, there is the opportunity available to make adjustments so that the risk event will not adversely affect the project. If a risk event happens, it is now a current or past event and is considered an issue and can be actively managed in the present. It is important to understand that what is a risk on one project or even in one work packet may not be considered a risk elsewhere. Companies have different risk tolerances that should be understood and documented when planning risk responses. Risk is generally thought to be a negative incident, however, it also could be a positive event. The inputs when performing Plan Risk Responses are the:

- Risk Management Plan
- Activity Cost Estimates
- Activity Duration Estimates
- Scope Baseline
- Stakeholder Register
- Cost Management Plan
- Schedule Management Plan
- Quality Management Plan
- Communications Management Plan

The processes mentioned above belong in the Planning Process Group and are overseen and monitored by the Monitor and Control Risk Process group.

Planning meetings and analysis should be the first order of business after the inputs have been gathered and recognized. The Risk Management Plan is an outline of the project's approach to risk. All Stakeholders should be included in the meetings and careful consideration should be taken when discussing and planning the approach to risk and the appropriate level of risk that will be tolerated on the project.

The meetings and analysis could include tools that we have discussed previously such as:

- Brainstorming sessions using open discussion within a group,
- The Delphi technique using questionnaires that solicit opinions from experts or deeply involved persons such as leads and workers who have experience with the work,
- Interviewing experienced participants, Stakeholders or subject matter experts to glean their experience and opinions, and
- Root Cause Analysis, attempting to determine underlying causes for any inherent risk.

Techniques used to determine risks to the project may include documentation reviews. Reviewing the documentation should provide insight into underlying causes for risks that may be recognized and mitigated. This also should lead to Assumptions Analysis, which is the exercise of challenging the assumptions made up to this point about the process and decision points. The assumptions may be incorrect or the plan and scope may have changed sufficiently to nullify or modify the assumptions.

Checklist analysis also should be used to ensure that no process, work packet or activity is missed in the planning or risk analysis stage. The list uses a Risk Breakdown Structure from the current or even previous projects to identify and help ensure that all significant risks or categories are evaluated.

To identify the **S**trengths, **W**eaknesses, **O**pportunities and **T**hreats to the project or to certain areas of the project, a SWOT analysis also should be used. Here again, the assumptions and beliefs in the SWOT analysis may have changed since the outset of the project. Throughout all of the analysis, expert judgment is needed and should be sought out for consultation.

Perform Qualitative Analysis

Qualitative Risk Analysis is the process by which the PM determines the "quality" of each risk identified in the previous exercises. Quality may sound like an odd term to use when talking about risk but there are two things to remember. First, each risk may be a negative OR a positive risk. Second, some risks are more likely to happen or may have a greater impact on the process and project. This is the process of qualifying the risks and judging their "quality" or their probability of occurring and their impact.

A Risk Probability Matrix is a great visual tool to use when qualifying risk. This matrix includes the probability of occurrence on one axis and the impact to the project on the other axis. The PM will assign values to probability and impact and where they intersect is a value. This value is the qualified risk value. The higher the number, the greater the risk (or

Douglas C. Ruh Jr.

opportunity).

To get started, the PM will obtain the Risk Register, Risk Management Plan, Project Scope Assessment and Organizational Process Assets Registers. These documents include accurate information about the risks and technical information, as well as the Management Plan, which is how are specific risks going to be handled. The Project Scope contains information the PM will need to determine the relative impact on the project and will serve to keep decisions made well within the boundaries of the project. The Organizational Process Assets Register outlines the organizational tools that the company has available to effectively manage and mitigate the risk.

When using these tools to place the values (probability and impact) of each risk, it is important to have the most current, accurate and unbiased information available so a risk data quality assessment should be performed to ensure data integrity and quality. Risks also should be evaluated and categorized into specific areas, such as the WBS or the RBS, indicating where the risk may take place and to which section it belongs. This is coupled with an urgency evaluation to determine the urgency of the risk. Will this risk happen tomorrow? Next week? Will it be during the closing exercises or be stayed to the next project, if it happens at all? Expert judgment should be applied to all of these review exercises, and the expert's biases about the risks should be noted and considered.

The Qualitative Risk Analysis has the effect of quickly identifying high priority risks. High priority, high urgency risks can be evaluated further if necessary in the next process as the risk is now part of the output, or deliverable.

While performing the analysis, the process will create Risk Register Updates as the output. These updates will be analyzed and become part of the updated Risk Register. The updates will most likely include a relative ranking scale with higher priority or impact risk near the top of the scale and require immediate attention. Lower impact or improbable risks are toward the bottom. The visual tool that is used is the Probability and Impact Matrix ranking. Grouping risks by category can illuminate risks that have an underlying common cause. Particular attention should be paid to grouping and identifying these areas and uncovering any underlying cause. Getting theses causes fixed may have the effect of removing a good portion of the risks from the register.

The PM should ensure that the Risk Rregister is prioritized with the most urgent or impactful risks needing immediate attention segregated at the top. Near term risks are tackled first. That's just good common sense.

Along with these risks should be a category for "more review needed" or "additional analysis" risks.

These are the type where more in-depth review and understanding is needed to accurately assess their impact. There should also be a low priority watch list. These are risks that might happen or have low impact on the project. During all of this categorization and placement of the risks, trend analysis should be performed. This exercise may uncover trends in the process that create risk or work areas that have unusual groupings of risks and is helpful in identifying trends and placing emphasis on areas that have higher occurrences of risk.

Perform Quantitative Analysis

Quantitative Analysis is a cousin to Qualitative Analysis. The two processes are very similar in that they analyze and classify risk. Quantitative departs from qualitative in that it is a deeper dive into the risks themselves. The PM is assessing a quality, a numeric value, to the risk. This is usually in the form of project costs or time.

The inputs are similar to those used in the qualitative process except the Cost Management Plan and the Schedule Management Plan is substituted for the Project Scope Assessment.

The quantitative process follows the qualitative process and may be optional if there are no risks that could be perceived to pose a substantial risk to the project's success. The Cost Management Plan contains information outlining the criteria for estimating, budgeting and controlling costs, therefore it will be useful if there is a process or activity that needs to be reviewed against planned costs. The Schedule Management Plan contains the same type of information that is specific to the scheduling process and is useful to determine if the schedule is realistic or needs to be adjusted to prevent failure.

What the PM is looking for are events or structural flaws that would indicate a failure (cost or time overruns) may be forthcoming or predicted and then determine an appropriate amount of funding that is necessary as a contingency plan.

The tools used to perform this more in-depth analysis are interviews, initially. Experienced professionals are always a good source of information when analyzing systems. Probability distributions are also tools that quantify the risks. The distributions usually assign a numeric value based on probability and impact. Usually, the higher the number on the scale, the more detrimental the effect will be.

A couple of good methods for evaluating risks with numeric values are the Expected Monetary Value Analysis (EMV) and the Decision Tree Analysis.

The EMV takes uncertain events and gives them a "most likely" monetary value. It assigns a cost. The costs are arrived at by assigning the probability of an uncertain event and the expected monetary impact of that event. The PM is looking for the proper amount of money to set aside as a contingency.

The Decision Tree is the method that the PM will most likely use to determine the root cause for an uncertain event. Once the root cause is identified, there are a series of options requiring decisions (thus, the decision tree) that must be made by the PM. Each decision is either optimistic or pessimistic and has a dollar value assigned. This guides the PM to make clear decisions based on risk tolerances, schedule and cost parameters. Throughout the process, expert judgment should be sought out and considered before finalizing this, the previous process and the output - the Risk Register Updates.

Plan Risk Reponses

Most people don't plan to fail, they fail to plan. This statement fits nicely here since Plan Risk Responses is planning to succeed by identifying possible failure events and planning an action or opportunity to correct such events.

Plan Risk Responses incorporate the Risk Management Plan and the Risk Register inputs. The Plan Risk Responses process creates a plan for handling each risk that presents itself. The Plan will be the last stop in the risk process, creating actionable responses to risk and assigning specific individuals to monitor and act on those risks. Specific tasks and responsibilities are assigned to specific team members. There are two categories of risk and each category has four possible responses tied to it that the individuals responsible will decide upon for each risk presented. One category is negative risks, or those risks that may adversely affect the project. The four responses for negative risks are:

Avoid. Avoidance is an appropriate response to risk. If a risk can be avoided with little or no residual effect, then it is a good choice to make. Going back to the cake and the flour choices, if we choose to use the fancy $9 flour, we risk blowing up the budget. To avoid this choice and use traditional all-purpose flour would be a good decision.

Transfer. Transferring risk is another manner of addressing risks. Transferring the risk makes it someone else's responsibility. Contractual agreements are one method to transfer risks. Have someone else bake the cake and risk using the expensive flour and your budget will be intact!

Mitigate. Mitigate means to make the risk less, to minimize the effects of the risk event. To do this, there may be other controls built into the process. This may include sourcing another flour market to mitigate the effects of having to use expensive flour.

Project Management. Simply Explained.

Accept. If the risk does present itself, it also acceptable to accept the risk, whether it is a positive or negative risk. Sometimes the focus is on the risk and in the big picture, the risk poses a minimal effect on the project. This would be a case of not seeing the forest through the trees. Some risks are OK to accept.

Positive risks are a category of risk that also have four basic strategies, similar to the negative risk categories.

Exploit. Yes, that's right, exploit! It may sound negative but it really just means to take advantage of the risk for the benefit it offers. Make sure that the benefit is received.

Share. Sharing the risk is used when the chances of the positive risk identified would be improved through collaboration with another department, company, etc. If sharing a project with another company would increase the chances that a big contract is secured, it is a positive risk to enter into the partnership.

Enhance. By understanding the underlying causes of a particular positive risk, the PM can enhance the chances of the risk happening. Once the causes are understood, the PM can take steps to trip the risk triggers and increase the likelihood that the risk will happen.

Accept. This strategy is virtually identical to the negative accept strategy except the nature of the risk is a positive influence on the project. Take the risk if you can, but don't go chasing after it.

The outputs for this process are the Risk Register Updates, which are specific updates to specific risk on the risk register.

Risk Related Contract Decisions is a document that addresses those risks that have been transferred to another party by way of contract. These contracts may mitigate risks by having another company that has specific expertise in an area perform the work, especially if the Sponsor company is lacking the expertise.

The Project Management Plan and the Project Document will be updated with changes to the budget, the schedule and the list of activities as called for. The documents created to list these changes and adjustments are the Project Management Plan Updates and the Project Document Updates.

4 RUNNING A PROJECT

Let's get cookin'. There has been, up to this point, a great deal of thinking, talking, negotiating and documenting in preparation for this grand project. The preparing and planning has been performed for this very moment. The moment that the project work commences. This is that time and now we discuss the hands-on production, creation and processes where the deliverables are created and completed.

Direct and Manage Project Execution

The planning, preparation and background work is now done and this is the process where the magic happens. The Direct and Manage Project Execution phase is where the actual project work starts. All of the planning that has been performed and all of the work plans detailed, communication channels, change request processes, parts, labor and personnel listings are now on full and public display. Very soon it will become apparent that the amount of planning that preceded production was either enough or not. As mentioned before, this is not an exercise in "firefighting," it is a structured, planned process that has used forethought and predictive modeling to ensure a smooth process. The planning is designed to prevent fires, not fight them. A planned project turns out a better product than an unplanned or "freelance" project.

The input documents that we have available for this process are the Project Management Plan, Approved Change Requests, Enterprise Environmental Factors and Organizational Process Assets. These are the basis of the project and contain the information needed to monitor and manage the execution of the many moving parts that a project has.

Project Management. Simply Explained.

Executing draws from five of the PMI knowledge areas and there are eight specific processes that are part of the Executing Process Group. These are:

- Direct and Manage Project Execution,
- Perform Quality Assurance,
- Acquire Project Team,
- Develop Project Team,
- Manage Project Team,
- Distribute Information,
- Manage Stakeholder Expectations, and
- Conduct Procurements.

Each of these processes has specific WBS Work Packages and Activities. As we can see, there is a lot to keep track of and manage. There are a lot of balls in the air, as they say. Understanding that there is a lot to start, perform and complete it is logical to assume that projects are disruptive. We need to keep in mind that all of this work, this project, is in addition to running the day-to-day business activities, many times with no (or very little) added human resources. The proper amount of planning will make the project easier. This aspect of the project relies heavily on the Monitor and Control process since we are starting production. We have learned that Monitor and Control is present in every aspect of the project phases, but it is particularly important now that production is at hand.

Part of the process that will inevitably occur is changes to the processes or to the activities or work packages. Any and all changes need to be formally requested and reviewed before they are accepted and put into effect. Changes have the effect of expanding or reducing the scope of the project and also can modify policies, procedures, costs, budgets and/or schedules. Since the scope may change, it is imperative to have the requested changes formally submitted and reviewed by the Change Control Board or the Stakeholder or Sponsor. The scope and project do not belong to the PM, rather to the Sponsor. Even though the changes may include corrective actions, prevent a possible difficulty, repair a defect or update the process, it is up to the OWNER of the project, the SPONSOR! The PM is only the caretaker of the project, not the owner.

Two topics to note are Configuration Management and Change Management. There is a difference between the two and the PM must understand the difference.

Configuration Management will focus specifically on the specifications of the deliverables and processes. The PM keeps an eye on new configurations that the deliverables are in need of, or that have been approved. They need to ensure that the new configuration will work within the scope and baselines that have been agreed upon by the Stakeholders and Sponsor. The configuration data, hierarchy and plans that are affected all must be updated and communicated across the Project Management team to ensure that they are understood and everyone involved has the most recent information.

Change Management focuses on modifying specific deliverables and processes. It is a more granular focus and affects individual processes and baselines. Macro and Micro. These are the basic differences between the focus of the two.

Perform Quality Assurance

Quality Assurance is about the process. It is not necessarily about the finished product. The PM should understand that the Quality Assurance process is about steadily improving the processes and activities that have been undertaken in the project process, with an eye on improving these processes. The idea is that with improved processes and activities, the product will inherently improve and cost savings will be realized to boot!

The main inputs are the Project Management Plan, which gives guidance on how the Perform Quality Assurance process will be executed. It also contains the Process Improvement Plan, which contains information about the work performed and how changes may be implemented to gain savings in cost, time or resources. Quality Metrics are also an important document since we are going to be measuring the process, improvements and metrics contained in the measurement data. Work Performance Information provides data and information about the work processes, both those that need attention and those that can be considered successes. Quality Control Measurements are part of a feedback loop of improvement information. When an improvement is made, the results are measured and fed back into Assurance and are the result of the quality control activities.

The tools that are used in the Plan Quality Assurance are the same as were used in the Plan Quality process and include Cost-Benefit analysis, Cost of Quality analysis, Benchmarking, Statistical Sampling and more.

Quality Audits are the key tool in this process because audits are the tools used for review of the process and where evaluation of the activities is performed. This allows objective assessment of what is working according to the Planned Quality expectations and what is not. Process Analysis is also essential to this process to ensure that the quality process is working efficiently, effectively and as designed.

Project Management. Simply Explained.

Acquire Your Project Team

Red rover, red rover, send Julie right over! As the PM on the project, you would like to think it is as easy as that to acquire your project team. And usually you would be mistaken.

The necessary inputs are the Project Management Plan, Enterprise Environmental Factors and the Organizational process assets. These inputs outline the activities to be completed (the plan) that determine the skills needed in these areas. They also determine what talent and skill sets are available in the organization (Enterprise Environmental Factors) as well as any specialized certifications (food safety, CPA, engineer). This also includes any specific laws or regulations, and other information necessary to the project that may be used in selecting the team. Finally, the Organizational Process Assets may have information, templates and lessons learned from other projects that may influence the team acquisition process. Getting down to business, it would be great to make a list of people the PM desires (wish list), hand it to the Sponsor and they say "absolutely, whatever you need!" This is not usually the case. There are many ways and channels that are available to assemble the team. We discuss some of them here.

Pre-assigned. This is a bit of a constraint but is certainly a workable situation. When a team is pre-assigned, there is the possibility that in the project charter, specialty employees are identified as a necessary element in the hiring process.

Negotiating is another method of acquiring qualified personnel for the project. Negotiations will be performed with the functional management staff. The PM will request certain individuals with specific skill sets for a defined period of time. This will give the functional manager a level of comfort that the employee will not be sucked into a black hole, never to be seen again until the project is completed. Remembering that a project is disruptive, the functional managers need to have reasonable assurances that their daily functions will not be disrupted unnecessarily.

Acquisition is another method of assembling the team. This method is usually used as a fill-in for missing or unavailable talent. It involves looking outside the firm for at-large individuals and bringing them in on a contract basis. This is not a substitute for using the firm's own employees. There may be valuable experience, networking or environmental expertise that the PM would forego at the chance to use company employees. Acquisition should be on an ad hoc basis when that is only the best choice.

Assembling Virtual Teams is a viable option using the available electronic media such as the Internet, email, conference calls and video conferencing. These tools allow disparate individuals to collaborate and communicate on activities, documents and deliverables. The plusses are that the PM can obtain qualified and productive team members. The minuses are that they may stay qualified, productive individuals and NOT become a team. Synergies may not form. This is no small thing and serious consideration should be given. The key notion when assembling the team is that the PM must focus on the skills needed, not the resources available, so flexibility and an understanding of the project and staff is important.

The outputs are the Project Staff assignments, which are the listing of the personnel resources that will be used in the project. The team members are each assigned to a role, or maybe several roles. Resource Calendars are another output that comes from the hiring process. The calendar outlines who will be working on what, and when. This allows each team member to know when they will be working on the assigned activities and allows Stakeholders and functional managers also to understand who is available for their regular work and who is currently working on the project activities.

Develop the Project Team

The reason that football teams have coaches is to develop the team's talent. The TEAM'S talent. A team works much better, more consistently with higher levels of quality than a group of individuals. Have you ever watched a college football team that had a bunch of new players? Then watched them three years later after the coaches have worked with them? Quite a difference! This is exactly what a good PM hopes to create in a very short amount of time.

The inputs are the Project Staff Assignments, which list all the team members and their assignments. The Project Management Plan is also included because it outlines the methods of training and how the project will be completed. This may include options that help build investment into the project with members of the team by offering benefits like flex time, overtime, telecommuting, etc. Resource Calendars are used because they detail when each individual will be working on specific activities. This also leaves open the opportunity for the PM to schedule team building exercises, one-on-one communication, etc.

Interpersonal skills are imperative for the PM to possess in order to build and develop the team. Happy and confident employees are more productive and agreeable than discontented employees. This is the reason that the PM's interpersonal skills will go a long way in helping the team members jell.

The PM should be sharing the vision for the project, motivating the team members. Interpersonal skills are not only rainbows and unicorns, though. The PM will define the ground rules, explain the scope and define the tasks. This builds trust, knowing where the boundaries are, what the expectations are and knowing that the PM is also approachable. They also will schedule training for employees who may need special skills. Training instills confidence and competence in the team members. Team building activities such as impromptu lunches, weekend excursions or other opportunities to lighten the atmosphere, create camaraderie and a sense of belonging and importance to the team and project.

Co-location is another method of building and developing the team. Teams who work in close proximity generally tend to interact more often, and more effectively than teams that are strewn about over several campuses or around the globe. These teams form bonds and create synergies that cannot be duplicated at a distance. These relationships and synergies may be the intangible that pushes the project from a "completed project" into the arena of "unmitigated success."

Recognition of achievement is a great method of instilling team building and confidence in the members. Win-win recognition is the best method of spotlighting achievement.

The personality makeup of the team is also important to the development of the team. The PM should be aware of the personalities and should not try and stock the pond with "cheerleaders and yes men." Skeptics add a certain dimension to the team because they see the downside. The opposite opinion can act to sharpen the process. Also, when others see 'ole sad sack getting on board with the project, they will be motivated to get involved, too.

The PM should expect to see Tuckman's phases while the team is congealing. These are the five phases:

- Forming,
- Storming,
- Norming,
- Performing, and
- Adjourning.

Let's touch on these phases for just a brief moment.

In the Forming stage, the individuals are new, may be timid and unsure, close minded. The PM needs to provide stability, structure and vision to the team. A clear direction needs to be communicated.

In the Storming stage the group usually experiences some conflict and power struggles. The project and innovation is top of mind and everyone wants to stake out their roles in the hierarchy. The PM's role is to continue to provide structure and stability within the team, keeping everyone focused on the goal and the project while negotiating differing opinions and points of view. It is also very important at this point that early accomplishments are recognized, to give the team a sense of accomplishment and pride.

The Norming stage usually sees the team starting to jell and work as a unit instead of individuals. There is trust in each other building and tempers, egos and opinions start to mellow. Habits are adjusted to benefit the team workflow and progress. The PM will begin to work in a facilitative style and loosen the reins a little, starting to share leadership roles with the group. As is justified and acceptable, the team shares more authority instead of having all of it reside with the PM. It's a good feeling now, isn't it? We are productive, trusted and working as adults.

Performing is the next stage and things are now running on all cylinders and there's high octane in the tank. The individuals are now functioning as team with a higher purpose, the project, instead of disparate motivations. The team members work together and problem solve together. The PM can now delegate some leadership responsibilities and focus more on refining the processes and making improvements.

Adjourning is the important last phase. It is important because of the investment the team members have had up to this point. They have given blood, sweat and tears for this project. Alas, the work is completed and the team must disband. This can be a big letdown for some. The PM will affirm the job is done and the performance achieved to the members of the team. There may be a formal ceremony, party, dinner or simply an impromptu meeting. The important part is that the PM closes out the project, releasing the employees while affirming their important contributions, and offering sincere thanks and a willingness to help them with a reference if requested.

As the PM, get to know your employees, what makes them tick. If you understand how they think and operate, their personality, strengths and weaknesses, you can communicate better and more effectively with them. There will inevitably be conflicts within the team; that is to be expected. Understand and anticipate team dynamics. If the PM has a conflict-free team, one would suspect that there are serious problems. Conflict, properly managed and directed, can produce great results, spur creative ideas, and create a healthy and competitive environment. All are good things in a team setting. The outputs for this process are Team Performance Assessments and Enterprise Environmental Factors.

Manage the Project Team

Managing the project team requires a deft touch, great amounts of high quality communication, and understanding personal and group dynamics. The inputs are Staff Assignments and the Project Management Plan. The output is the Develop Team phase.

Managing the team goes back to people skills. The biggest part of managing the team is communicating effectively, showing leadership, conflict management and negotiating skills with the team members. Tracking activity and employee performance and making accurate assessments is a necessary task. This allows the PM to monitor issues and conflicts, and to make adjustments and improvements while the issues are still small and manageable.

Managing also involves ensuring that the team members have the right amount of work to perform. Too much assigned and the team member feels overworked and incapable. Too little and there is not enough production and they lose interest and become bored. It can be a fine balancing act.

When forced to enter into conflict management, the PM can use a number of different methods. They will need to know which to use with different employees. They range from simply walking away, retreating, to confrontation and solving the conflict right then and there. In between are accommodating, compromising and collaborating, all various levels of working together. All can be effective if administered to the right person in the right situation.

Interpersonal skills cannot be overlooked here. The PM must display leadership and inspire the team. Sharing the project and team vision is important. When the PM is constrained by the Sponsor or Stakeholders, they will be able to be an influencing force, persuading and cajoling them into agreement. They will rely on persuasive logic to bolster their influence which means that they will have to learn important points and priorities. They also will need to be informed about every aspect of the team, the project and the corporate culture.

Active listening skills and the ability to weigh different courses of logic, opinions and methods will be useful skills to incorporate.

Part of managing the team and incorporating the skills and attributes we just touched on is how the PM interacts with team members. The PM should be visible and approachable. To set this tone, the PM should personally hand out the work assignments, taking time to explain the deliverables for each activity and work packet. Due dates need to be clearly communicated and with that, the level of effort needed to complete the activity on time must be communicated clearly as well. Any potential obstacles or extenuating circumstances also will be discussed. There should be clear and concise communication. This will create open and effective communication and build confidence in the PM and the team.

Managing the team involves communicating on a regular basis, not just at the kickoff meeting. The PM should speak with every team member on a regular basis; keep communication regular and open. This does not mean scheduling a meeting every week, month, etc. A water cooler discussion can produce incredible results. A key to successful individual communications is knowing the team member's assignments and their abilities. They may be a little underwater, needing a little help or advice, or they may just feel overwhelmed. Knowing their ability and activity will tell the PM if there is reason for concern. Active listening is a key skill when communicating. The team members know when the PM is shining them on so don't do it. Your success depends upon the job they do. Listen and react appropriately. After all, it is your job to make them productive.

Team meetings are a method to keep the team on track as a whole. The project overview can become clearer to the team members in meetings. The PM should make sure that the goals are stated, both short and long term, and what progress has been made in achieving them.

If there have been intermediate achievements, they should be discussed and celebrated. Remaining goals will be aligned with the project and barriers to completion discussed in the meetings. Everything should be on the table so that there are no surprises. If there are activities that a team member volunteers to perform but really lacks the tools to complete, the PM is responsible. They should know the skill set needed and if it is not a match, find the right one. It is the PM's duty to manage the team and mismatching abilities and activities is not managing effectively. Lastly, keep the meetings concise.

To conclude, when managing the team, the PM should maintain the strategic vision and keep the near term goals aligned. The PM sets the "tone at the top" and that tone should include continuous learning and sharing knowledge, opinions and experiences with the team. That tone also should contain flexibility in the PM's management style and paying attention to the team members, drawing them into the team culture, and keeping them invested in the project.

Manage Stakeholder Expectations

The Rolling Stones wrote, "You can't always get what you want, but if you try sometimes, you just might find, you get what you need."

Managing Stakeholder Expectations is the process that manages just these times. The purpose of Managing Stakeholder Expectations is to influence their expectations, especially if after the project starts they express pie in the sky expectations. I'm sure we all have been on a project, decided on a result and then, halfway into the project, Mr. or Ms. Creativity comes up with six new and better ways to finish the project. This is what the PM is doing in this process, managing expectations. Keeping our eyes firmly affixed to the scope and baselines and letting the Stakeholders know how close to plan the project is progressing.

If the PM is closely aligned with the goals and understands the benefits and risks of straying too far versus holding tight to the course, they can increase the likelihood of project acceptance in the end. Isn't that what it's all about? The PM, by maintaining a constant eye on the plan and goals, will be able to see any problems in the distance and will be able to devise workarounds, fixes or even scope, or plan changes (approved by the Sponsor) in time to avoid the plan becoming unbalanced.

By addressing their concerns before they know that they have concerns, it will avert a negative impact on the project.

When these situations present themselves, the issues are corrected in a timely manner and tracked on the Issue Log. If the PM can determine the reaction of the Stakeholder, chances are there will be an amicable resolution and the Stakeholder will maintain confidence and the PM will avoid a negative experience or negative impact on the project.

The first step is identifying the Stakeholders and understanding their needs concerning the project. This is particularly important because if the PM doesn't understand who the Stakeholders are and what their needs are, there is little chance they can be successful. Technically, maybe the project is completed, but are the Stakeholders and Sponsor satisfied? If not, the project might not be considered a success.

Identifying the Stakeholders is one of the first jobs that the PM will undertake. They should create a Stakeholder Register to identify the Stakeholders, their investment in the project, at what stage they are invested and their level of authority in the company. Classifying the Stakeholders in this manner will help create communication channels as the project commences and proceeds from production to close.

The Stakeholder Register is an input that can lend understanding of the Stakeholders involved and their interest in the project. The Procurement Documents also will help identify Stakeholders of a different sort. These are the contractors on the project who also have an interest in the project and are by definition, Stakeholders.

As part of the Stakeholder Register the PM also will create a Stakeholder Analysis. This is an analysis of the identified Stakeholders and their level of authority and need for level and type of communication. This also should contain a little bit of "personality type" information about the Stakeholders. This information will most likely prove to be an indispensable ally when managing the Stakeholders. This will be the PM's private guide as to HOW to present information to get the best result from the Stakeholders, good or bad.

The PM will create a Stakeholder Management Strategy and this will be a closely held document, not published with the rest of the project documents. This "personal" document should identify those Stakeholders who will benefit from the project and those who may have negative intentions for the project. It is important to realize that not everyone will be excited about the project and potential changes it will bring. Some may see the project as possibly eliminating their job and not take too kindly to that notion. The PM should identify the Stakeholders with positive intentions and capitalize on their enthusiasm and participation to move the project along and maximize their efforts. In contrast, those that have been identified as having a possible negative should be mitigated.

Stakeholder Management is a strategy that takes deliberate forethought and planning if the PM is going to manage all Stakeholders effectively.

The Project Management Plan, Issue Log and Change Log are all documents that will help to crystallize the PM's position and provide backup documentation for requesting changes, thereby helping to mitigate the Stakeholder's response.

We have talked a bit about the methods of communication by personality type, level of involvement, rank in the company and so on. The

Project Management. Simply Explained.

main point in managing Stakeholders is that communication should be face-to-face whenever possible, using your best interpersonal and communication skills. If it seems impossible, make it happen. Then, follow up with written documents restating your discussion and any alternatives discussed. Face-to-face communication imparts a respect to the Stakeholder, letting them know that they are important enough to contact personally. This builds trust and relationships. This is managing Stakeholders.

Conduct Procurements

The procurement process is a four-step process, conducting procurements being the second step in the process. The four steps are:

- Plan Procurements. The outputs are the Procurement Management Plan and the Procurements Statement of Work.
- Conduct Procurements. The outputs are Selected Sellers and Procurement Contract Awards.
- Administer Procurements. The outputs are the Procurement Documentation and Change Requests.
- Close Procurements. The output is the Closing Procurements document.

The process is and should be a formal and structured process in Project Management. Most of us in the workplace have limited experience with procurements that look something like this: We need something to complete our work such as a ream of paper to print our report, new pencils, sticky notes, etc. We "procure" the supplies from the supply cabinet or the stockroom. Simple, huh? Now on a project with many individuals needing all kinds of resources to complete the activities we can just imagine how cost overruns and duplication of efforts and supplies will throw the cost, timing and quality of the project off. Since the "supplies" may be computer programs or even completed deliverables supplied by outside companies, we can see just how important it is to manage the procurement process effectively and efficiently.

Planning Procurements is the step preceding the Conduct Procurements process. The project requirements should be thought out in advance. Procurements in the project management world are more than just pencils and sticky notes. They involve deciding what activities and deliverables can and should be created in-house and which should be contracted out or procured. The inputs for the process are nearly everything! They include the Scope Baseline, Requirements Documentation, Teaming Agreements, Risk Register, Activity Resource Requirements, Project Schedule, Activity Cost Estimates, Cost Performance Baseline, Enterprise Environmental Factors, Organizational Process Assets and sometimes the kitchen sink. OK, maybe not the kitchen sink.

Now that the PM has the needed information they must determine what needs to be procured. This is a make or buy decision. While that does not seem too complicated, the wrong decision could seriously imperil the project. There are a ton of considerations to be made, including risk to the company, the corporate culture (they may have an in-house construction leaning), legal entanglements with suppliers, timing of needed resources and deliverables, etc. This planning should be done as early in the process as is feasible. Sometimes it is just not possible to have all the procurement decisions made before the work starts. The good news is that the procurement process can be performed throughout the project when needed.

Early on in our cake project the PM recognized that frosting for the cake can be made from scratch with sourced raw ingredients or it can be purchased in a little tub, pre-made and available in the grocery store and applied by a frosting specialty company. The cost to make it from scratch may be double or more the cost of the pre-made frosting. The pre-made frosting has 20 ingredients, many are difficult to pronounce and while it does taste acceptable, it does not have the "pop" that scratch frosting has, with its four (pronounceable) ingredients. Both will do the job of completing a deliverable. This is where it becomes a little tricky and expert judgment must be used. Does the Sponsor want in-house resources used? Do they want the more natural and controllable product? Is cost savings the primary driver? Is this a skill that is not readily available in-house and should be procured? Do they want to have this skill cultivated and available in-house? With this many questions arising just from the "frosting conundrum," can you imagine what is involved in creating a software program or constructing a building?

After the PM engages in the make-or-buy analysis, taking into consideration not only cost and timing, but the company's other interests that may come into play such as gaining proficiencies in certain production processes, they are generally ready to put feelers out for contracts. It must be mentioned emphatically that there will be an immense amount of expert judgment applied throughout the analysis.

The Conduct Procurement process involves contracting resources and finished deliverables with other sources. Several types of contracts may be entered into, each with positive and negative points inherent. It is prudent to give mention of the different types of contracts and their attributes. The first and easiest to understand is a **Lump Sum** or **Fixed Price** contract. The basic element here is that there is a fixed price, defined scope and completion date. The risk is transferred to the seller. There are variations including one with an incentive for say, early completion. The incentive may be in the form of a bonus payment. Also available are fixed price with an economic price adjustment. This is to offset differences in currency fluctuations, cost of living adjustments, etc.

Cost reimbursable contracts are structured so that the costs for completion are transferred back to the buyer upon delivery. This will include a small profit margin if it is a **Cost Plus Fixed Fee** contract. If it is a **Cost Plus Incentive** contract, there could also be a bonus for early completion.

Time and Materials contracts are just as they sound. They are payable for cost of time and materials. Usually there is a markup on the materials and may include a slight premium on the time, or labor.

Contracts are legal and binding documents that the companies are entering into and should be written by someone with experience in this area whether it is a contract specialist or the company's legal team. The PM should most likely abstain from writing and agreeing to the contract without a great deal of expert judgment.

Conduct Procurements. We have our requirements figured out and are now in the market to purchase the needed resources. Typically there is a process involved that looks something like this. A request for information, quote or proposal is submitted. There may be a bidders conference in which bids are received and reviewed. The suppliers in the conference all receive the same project information and parameters including cost, quality, timing, etc., allowing them to make their best proposals with all the information on the table for everyone to see. This makes a level playing field during the process. Proposals are drawn up suggesting which bid to accept and the reasons why it is acceptable. An evaluation of the bid(s) takes place with the appropriate Stakeholders and if there are no objections, a proposal is accepted and a contract is tentatively awarded. Now the contract is negotiated (finer details) with the supplier and when all the details are ironed out, a contract is agreed upon and signed. It is worth stating again that expert judgment is critical and should be an integral part of this process.

There are a number of ways to gather bids and proposals for the needed components. We mentioned a bidders conference in which the bidders are all making their best pitches and they are all on a level playing field. The PM also may solicit independent estimates from a company or group that specializes in this activity. This is known as a "should cost" estimate and gives the PM a baseline for what the market should be charging. Advertising is another means of soliciting bids and proposals. The local newspaper or trade journal may be a viable alternative to the phone book and can produce excellent results. Internet searches are all the rage but may not produce the desired results, therefore more traditional channels are still preferred.

The output is the Selected Sellers listing. This is simply confirmation that the company has selected a supplier and is entering (or has entered) into a relationship with the identified seller.

The other output is the Procurement Contract Award. This is usually in the form of a formal contract that specifies the relationship between the company and the supplier, items like cost, due dates, quality level, incentives and other details of the relationship. This is usually highly detailed in structure and is a legal and binding document that requires a great deal of expert judgment, usually in the form of a legal practitioner. The contract also will include a claims and dispute resolution process clearly spelling out the grievance process and jurisdiction.

Resource Calendars are another output and are updated with the new dates when the contract deliverables will be received so that everyone can anticipate the in-house work yet to be performed. This allows the PM to keep the project on schedule. Change requests, Project Management Plan updates and Project Document updates are also outputs that are created and updated as needed. The remaining two functions in the procurement process, Administering and Closing Procurements, will be discussed a little later.

5 MONITORING AND CONTROL

Monitor and Control Project Work

Monitor and Control Project Work focuses on the differences between the baselines and the current project. The PM is constantly comparing where we are with where we should be. This is a fancy way of saying that the PM is simply making sure that the plan is working. If things are not working as they are supposed to, then the PM will suggest course corrections or changes to the Sponsor to get the project back on track.

The inputs are the Project Management Plan and the Performance Reports, as well as the Enterprise Environmental Factors and the Organizational Process Assets.

Using the inputs as guidelines, the PM monitors the work group's progress against the scheduled timelines and milestones. Efforts during this process are concentrated on recognizing where the project and activities are slipping and then planning corrective actions to bring the work and efforts back in line with the plan. Alternatively, if the plan was overly optimistic, the PM will request changes to the plan and present them to the Sponsor for discussion and hopefully, approval. This is all about the ability to track performance and monitor progress. If you can't track variances in the processes, you don't have a good plan.

When the changes are approved they are implemented and monitored by the PM. Updated forecasts of the project completion dates and costs are also recalculated and presented, becoming part of the most current baseline. Since the change requests are all documented as discussed earlier, they become part of the Plan Document in the Change Request ledger. This applies to all change requests, approved or denied. It is important to ensure that the requests are all preserved so that when the PM looks back and evaluates the project, the change request outcomes are available to study and possibly be used in upcoming projects. They also provide justification of the project's outcomes, including deliverables timing, cost and labor. Although monitoring and tracking is looking back at performance it is also, and more importantly, about looking forward and influencing future results. It is not just fixing past mistakes. After all, the project continues to move forward and so must we.

To summarize this process, we can look at monitoring and controlling as two functions; The first is monitoring, consisting of analyzing the performance data. This includes collecting, measuring and distributing performance data to the appropriate Stakeholders. The PM needs to be able to assess the information and look for trends that may be emerging. Trends that are identified allow the PM to take appropriate corrective action. Trend analysis helps highlight any areas or processes that need additional attention.

Controlling is the second half and consists of determining the correct actions to take for individual weaknesses or emerging trends and may require re-planning. Controlling is not completed only by determining the corrective actions needed. The PM also ensures that the new plans are implemented and completed.

Verify Scope

Think product or project comparison, not accuracy. When the PM verifies the scope or verifies most anything, it is against a standard, a measurement. In the case of verifying the scope, the PM is comparing the plan with the results. Fairly straightforward on its face, but it can become a bit tricky when production starts. Let's face it, when was the last time you tried to undertake a "project" that went without a hitch? Something unexpected always seems to happen. It's Murphy's Law! Project Management is no exception. It's usually bigger than baking a cake.

Verify Scope is part of the Scope Management process. This process also includes Collect Requirements, Define Scope and Create WBS that we have already touched on. The remaining two processes are Verify and Control Scope, which conveniently are this subject and the next.

Verify Scope is really a process of comparing the deliverable to the scope and making sure they match. It is a similar process to Perform Quality Control. Many times it is performed at the same time, but it may be

Project Management. Simply Explained.

performed after Quality Control.

Although most of us would ask "aren't they doing the same thing?" The answer is no, not really. Quality Control is generally concerned with correctness, that is, are all the pieces included? Does it look like the prototype? Does it look, smell, taste or sound like it is intended to?

Verify Scope on the other hand concerns itself with questions like did we miss any steps? Did we make sure all of the processes and activities were performed? Does it match the plan (scope) and not include or exclude anything? Can we show the Stakeholders that this deliverable is what they planned and they will find it acceptable? The difference may seem subtle but it is really significant.

The acceptance of the deliverable by the Sponsor is the milestone that we are shooting for here. After all, Sponsor acceptance is the ONLY reason we are performing this project, right?

Verify Scope is usually performed after some deliverables are completed so that there is something to compare to the Scope Baseline. Verification can be performed many times throughout the project, as needed. It is usually conducted fairly late in the game since deliverables are needed to verify.

The input that is usually needed is the Project Management Plan, since logically it is a plan of the project. It contains the Scope Baseline and the WBS and WBS dictionary. The baseline is the measurement device that the PM will use to verify the deliverables against since it was created as the plan for the deliverable and is the objective standard to measure against.

The Requirements Documentation is a listing, or log, of the project requirements that the Stakeholders have created. This is their thoughts and feelings about the deliverable and will provide good source of information about the project.

The Requirements Traceability Matrix links the individual requirements to the Stakeholder who created, requested and submitted them. This is nice to have in case there is a question about the requirement, why it is inserted and needed. If a change needs to be made the logic behind the decision would be useful in finding an acceptable work around and still maintaining the original integrity of the Stakeholder's requirements.

Validated Deliverables is the last input. The deliverables are compared to the scope to ensure that everything is complete and no steps were missed in the process. Make sure it is good to go.

Inspection is the tool that is used to ensure that the deliverable meets scope requirements. A point-by-point comparison to the scope is made between the deliverable and the Scope Document. Hands-on testing by the Sponsor or Stakeholders is also acceptable as inspection. If the deliverable was a software program, an alpha or beta copy delivered for testing would be an example.

The outputs are the Accepted Deliverables, Change Requests and Project Document Updates. The Accepted Deliverables are the primary output since it is the documentation that the deliverable met expectation and now the Sponsor is taking delivery, satisfied that the deliverable is within the scope and expectations.

Change Requests should be an accepted reality for any project. Change Requests are formal and have consequences. The consequences, good or bad, need to be documented and made a part or the project so that the Sponsor can see what changes were requested, accepted or rejected, and what the results were. This is particularly useful when presenting the Sponsor with the deliverable. The PM is able to show the completed deliverable was verified against the scope and the baseline. Also, they are useful when reevaluating the project and are lessons learned when starting up a new, similar project.

The next three items - scope, schedule and cost - are intertwined and are considered a part of the Performance Measurement Baseline. This baseline includes all three and the PM is obligated to monitor and control each, even though they are separate entities. This is the "maintaining project balance" that we discussed earlier. If one of the three changes, those changes will affect at least one of the other two, thereby throwing the project out of balance.

My grandfather once described a milking stool and its ingenious three legged design. The three legs provided stability and was more suited to a barn environment than a four-legged stool. It is simply easier to balance three-legged stools than four-legged stools on the barn floor, making it easier to "Perform the Milking Process." How easy would it be to maintain balance if we cut 1 inch off of one leg? I can imagine that milking would be difficult without a stable place to sit and conduct our activity. The stool needs to be brought back into balance. A change request is submitted, approved and we cut an inch off of the remaining two legs. Presto! Our change is implemented, our activity can be completed and we have a delicious deliverable to enjoy with our cake!

Project Management. Simply Explained.

Control Scope

Scope creep is a PM's worst nightmare. Scope creep or scope expansion is the phenomenon of adding little bits (or sometimes big bits) to the scope to "improve" the deliverable. As Nancy Reagan said, "Just say no." Say no as often as possible or the project will quickly spin out of control and become unbalanced. Remember the milking stool? The PM has a scope that they are hired to work by. This includes a budget; deliverables, descriptions and requirements; costs, labor and work packets; as well as human resources that all have permanent homes. If changes to the scope are allowed to creep into the project, everything else is affected. Let's not make the mistake that the scope cannot change, only that it should be a difficult and deliberate process to change it. Certainly there will be disagreements and arguments about when and why scope or requirements are needed. Any scope changes that are considered should be done with the lean to making the Sponsor happy.

The inputs to the Control Scope process are the Project Management Plan, the Work Performance information, Requirements Documentation, Requirements Traceability Matrix and the Organizational Process Assets.

Just to briefly revisit these inputs (since these were discussed in Chapter 3), the Project Management Plan and Requirements Documentation tell us what steps are involved in the project and when they should be taken, as well as what the deliverable should look like and what attributes it should have. The Traceability Matrix allows the PM to go straight to the individual who created or first documented the requirement, which is very useful for maintaining the original deliverable integrity in the face of changes.

Control Scope is concerned with making sure that all of the scope requirements are worked through and met. This means only APPROVED requirements that have gone through the change process and were given the green light. Again, this "control" function tries to ensure that the scope is the guiding principle and that variances from the scope are what is being monitored.

Variance Analysis is a great method and the tool used for identifying the variances between the work and the scope. This also can illuminate and identify trends and measure the magnitude of difference from the scope by tracking the requested changes and their results. If the results are not meeting expectations, steps such as education, one-on-ones or any manner of process improvements can be undertaken.

The output for the Control Scope process is the Work Performance Measurements, which is important because it is a key to understanding the work performance data that was actually recorded against the scheduled scope. This may be a revelation that can be used in other areas of the project, or on different projects. Organizational Process Asset Updates are also important to record and retain because they may reveal that the Project Scope Management Plan has been inadequate from the start.

Change requests. We have beaten this into the red Georgia dust, haven't we? Project Management Plan Updates must be recorded, implemented and monitored.

Control Schedule

It's all about timing. Really, it is! This is the part of the project that endeavors to keep it on time, and is part of the Time Management process. It is a "monitor and control" process and really should start as soon as the schedule is adopted and accepted. It lasts throughout the project, until close. The PM should be comparing the work completed against the schedule to maintain a comfort level that the work is being performed and the schedule is not in danger.

Changes in the schedule affect many parts of the project from supply chain to human resources availability, so it is important to ensure that the schedule is not disrupted excessively. The PM should be scanning the horizon for difficulties that may throw the schedule off, proactively affecting the situations trying to head off changes to the schedule.

Schedule changes should be planned out and evaluated against the baseline and completion date.

As part of the Project Management Plan, there is the Schedule Management Plan and the Schedule Baseline that will be the primary input since it has the project and schedule plans. This document also outlines the change process and the management process.

As situations arise that necessitate changes to the schedule, change requests go through the change process and once approved, they are integrated and the schedule is updated.

The inputs are the Project Management Plan, the Project Schedule, Work Performance information and Organizational Process Assets.

The tools that are used to monitor and control the schedule are performance reviews, which show the planned start and finish dates of each activity and WBS. These tools are used by the PM in their effort to analyze the variances between current spending on the project against planned spending, right down to the work package and activity levels if necessary. The performance reviews show the activity progress against the plan. It is logical to assume that if there is a delay in production, there will be extra costs associated with the activity. No one will be working for free to finish the activity, therefore there is at least the added cost of additional labor. There also may be additional materials costs. Variance Analysis is a tool that is helpful for the PM to understand where and especially why an activity or a work package has veered off course, or if there is a trend emerging. There may be an overly aggressive schedule, a labor dispute, lack of necessary resources or any other number of problems that crop up. The key is to identify them, get out in front of them and find a reasonable solution.   It may include reevaluating the project scope or dipping into reserves to bring more resources to bear on the project for a time.

One of the tools a PM has to correct variances is Project Management software, which simplifies the task of analysis.   Once the analysis is performed, the corrective actions may include resource leveling - simply ensuring that the correct number of resources are allocated across the entire project.   If resources are thrown into one activity to bring it into line, another activity may have a problem because of that action. Now the PM is in the same predicament only in a different area.

What if scenarios are useful in "brainstorming" different methods of aligning the plan with the reality. They may come up with an innovative solution to the problem.   Adjusting leads and lags to reflect the current workflow situation is another method of controlling the schedule and ensuring that the project comes in on time. Using a scheduling tool to help manage the schedule and the costs associated with the plan and actual schedule variances is always a good thing. Trying to calculate the data manually is time-consuming and costly, and may not be the most accurate method.   A scheduling tool will allow the PM to realistically consider whether "crashing" an activity or two makes sense or if they can benefit from schedule compression.

Using an Earned Value Management technique will allow the PM to have a good idea of the project status as it integrates the scope, cost and schedule measures into a nice and tidy report.   Combining these three important areas will allow a complete picture of the status. Using only one of the three criteria could be misleading. If the schedule shows that the work package is on time, that's great right? What if it is over cost and steps have been skipped to try and correct the cost overrun? Now it is out of scope. By combining the three areas, there is a less likely chance that these will be missed. Forecasting and providing an updated estimate of costs at completion is another tool that can be used. This will let the PM and any Stakeholders know far in advance if there will be cost overruns. This can be performed throughout the project if desired.   This is similar to performing a To-Complete Performance Index that calculates the projected costs from that specific point in the project to completion for the remaining work. This will give the PM a good idea if the cost goal that management set out initially (or updated) will be accomplished. All are very good tools that provide the PM with a look forward.

In short, controlling the schedule is important because the PM has a dedicated delivery date and the Sponsor and Stakeholders are all counting on the project to follow the schedule.   Most of the participants in the project have "day jobs" and need to get back to them. Remembering that a project is extracurricular to their regular duties and is disruptive goes a long way to help remind us of the reasons that a schedule is necessary. Additionally, when a schedule gets a little out of whack, it throws other things out of whack, including labor, resources, parts and supplies timing, etc. All cost money. This brings us to controlling the costs.

Control Costs

"A penny saved is a penny earned." Benjamin Franklin wrote this about personal finances but it seems to me to fit into the PM world as well, especially in the Control Costs process.

Controlling costs is the process of ensuring that the project does not run over budget (or too far under budget). Controlling costs can be thought of as the purest form of controlling a project. Everything has a cost associated with it such as, labor, supplies, information and time. The PM is aware that controlling costs controls everything else.

When performing Controlling Costs, the PM will look for variances between the actual costs and the planned costs or the cost baseline. This will happen almost immediately since projects start to incur costs immediately. The PM themselves are a cost, after all.

Variance can be in either a the positive or negative direction when compared to the baseline, or schedule. Negative variances indicate that the project is leaking funds, that something is not quite right and costs are more than expected. This observation should be addressed immediately and the project put back on a sturdy footing. Positive variances also should be addressed. An astute PM will not just rejoice in the idea that money is saved. Find out why. Maybe an activity has been missed.

Controlling Costs is not a one-off process. As we discussed earlier, it is done early and often.

Initially, during kickoff or the initiation phase, the PM can be a little more relaxed about it but as production ramps up and more activity is ongoing, frequent analysis is warranted.

The Project Management Plan and the Project Funding requirements are important inputs. These documents outline in detail the Cost Performance Baseline and the Cost Management Plan. The baseline details how much things are scheduled to cost, and the management plan details how the costs will be managed.

Additionally, the Work Performance Information and Organizational Process Assets are inputs that have information concerning the performance of the teams currently engaged in the activities. This is compared to the baseline to determine if there are variances and how much cost differential the variances are creating. There also may be some applicable information from other projects, standards and guidelines, company policies and such that can be used to guide the process back into compliance with the baseline.

One of the tools that the PM has at their disposal are the Earned Value Management reports. This is simply a set of reports that combines the scope, cost and schedule measurements to give a value against the combined baselines, combining all three legs of the stool to make sure they are balanced.

The Earned Value Measurement is a measurement that combines all three (scope, cost and schedule) because the assumption is that any activity adds *value* to the project. The variance will be if there is more or less value than planned.

Forecasting is also a tool that the PM will use to determine how close to delivering on time, in scope and on budget the project will be. The keys here are the Estimate at Completion and Estimate to Completion reports. These are fairly straightforward. Estimate to Completion is an assessment of funds needed from the current point of the project in order to complete the project. The "at completion" report is the lump sum at the end.

There are index reports that also can be used to give an indication of the project's standing. The To Complete Performance Index (TCPI) measures the performance needed, using the Earned Value, that it will take to complete the project for a specific discipline, such as a specific budget.

Performance reviews also play a part in indicating cost variances. As we covered before, everything costs money. In the business world, labor is a manager's biggest controllable. If the performance is inadequate, there might be a need for higher quality labor. Get more done with less labor.

The outputs are the work performance measurements that detail how the project is coming along. These are reviewed by the PM and interested Stakeholders. Included would most likely be the Cost Variance, Schedule Variance and the associated index reports.

Budget forecasts also are created as an output. These forecasts let the Sponsor and Stakeholders know where the project stands and that all the legs are in balance (or not). If there will be more money needed, they should know sooner rather than later.

Additional outputs that we have discussed before but need to be mentioned here are the Organizational Process Assets and any additions to it. Change Requests also will be logged and become a permanent part of the project documentation, as well as any Plan Management Plan and Project Document updates. Remember, all actual and proposed changes are recorded.

And there we have the three legs of the stool and how to keep them all the same length so that the PM does not fall off and spill our milk.

Douglas C. Ruh Jr.

Perform Quality Control

Perform Quality Control is the process by which the *deliverable* is under scrutiny, not so much the process. This process is undertaken continually throughout, not just once or twice.

To perform quality control, the product is generally tested and inspected, and the most common method is statistical sampling to determine if the product or deliverable meets the quality standards set by the Stakeholders and Sponsor.

The Project Management Plan and the details of how quality control will be carried out are used as the input document. The plan is now in the PM's hands. Quality Metrics, Quality Checklists and Work Performance Measurements assess dimensions of technical detail and specifications that are integral and necessary to consider the product a quality success. The Checklist also is utilized so that nothing is missed in the process. Approved change requests also are obtained as an input because it never hurts to know what standards and specifications or processes and activities have changed and are now considered current before they are tested. The deliverables are the main input into this process because it is the deliverables that are being inspected, tested and judged for conformity to quality standards. Although the deliverables are the primary focus, it is important to understand that the process also is similarly being evaluated as well. The process after all is what will make the deliverable acceptable or not.

To test the process and the product, there are a variety of tools that the PM has at their disposal. Cause and Effect or Ishikawa (fishbone) diagrams are a helpful tool used to trace back the process to find root problems. This is a look back from the finished product to the point where the defect was perpetrated. It looks like a fishbone and, much like a 3-year-old, helps the PM to ask why, why, why, until a suitable answer is obtained.

Control Charts, flow charts and histograms are all various tools to help define the frequency of defects, the levels of defects in relation to control estimates and expectations, and the process flow or activities that are charted to help identify choke points or known timing or workload issues.

Inspection is just that, inspecting the deliverable. Whether it is a basketball, cake, building, car or software program, this is where it is time to kick the tires, take a taste or a test drive, or run the program.

The outputs are Quality Control Measurements, Validated Changes and Validated Deliverables. It is important to take and record the quality control measurements so that past and future performance can be analyzed and improvements realized and made. Validated changes happen when defects are detected and changes are made to remedy the defect. The change and the results must be documented and validated to ensure they had the desired result. Deliverables are validated and are the key output of this step. This validating helps ensure that the deliverables pass inspection and meet quality standards.

Manage Communications

Managing Communications includes distributing information and reporting performance, two unique topics that have been melded into one with the newest version of the PMBOK® (v5).

To start, distributing information is all about how to get the information to those that need it in a manner that is best for all parties.

There are three main types of communication modes and each has its strengths and weaknesses. The first is "push" mode. This is "pushing" information to the intended recipients. "Pull" communication requires the recipient to actually pull the information in, say from a website or an Internet/intranet source. This is usually best for very large audiences. The third, and the one most are familiar with, is the "interactive" method, where two or more parties exchange ideas, thoughts and such back and forth. Interactive communication helps ensure there is mutual understanding and agreement between parties, whereas with either push or pull communication, there is no such guarantee that the message was understood, much less received.

Different communication tools are used for different purposes and for different audiences. The PM should be aware of what type and how much information is needed by which Stakeholder.

An Executive Status Report is a type of push communication that is mainly for upper level management. Think Sponsor. Upper-level executives like to have their reports easily digestible in just a few minutes. By few, we mean five or so. One-page printed reports are a favorite of most executives as are dashboard-type electronic reporting that gives an overview of agreed-upon critical areas. The executive will always dig deeper or ask more questions if they want more information, but they will not dig through paragraphs of "fluff" to get to the pertinent information. The information in the executive reports is concerned with variances from the Baseline and Scope, the three legs of the stool. The executives simply want to know if the project is in balance, and if not, how is it going to be brought back into balance.

Team status reports are different in that they are a little more oriented toward the goals that are before the team currently. They are a little more interactive and user-involved, purposefully, since they are reporting on team performance, goals and the distance to the finish line. These reports focus on the causes for variance and remedies to overcome the variance. Goals for the next reporting period also are part of the communication. This communication is used as a motivational and team building tool as well as a status report for the teams. The desirable styles are face-to-face whether in person or virtual, such as a video conference. The information is immediate, acknowledged and confirmed as received. It is personal and invests the team member at a personal level as well.

Reporting information, the granular detailed information, the nuts and bolts, is a choice that is left up to the PM and management. There are a number of formats that distribute information to different levels of Stakeholders, including scatter charts, histograms, milestone charts and dashboards to name a few. Some companies like information saturated with charts and reports, others like the slim facts. The key point is, use whatever format that delivers the information and will be received well by the Stakeholders.

Performance, whether good or bad, needs to be reported to the Stakeholders on a regular basis. How regular depends on the level of the Stakeholder. Team members working on individual activities may benefit from daily stand-ups (informal, short meetings where the participants are gathered together and stand up), or memos or weekly updates, whereas the Sponsor may only require an executive summary once a week or less.

The lesson to be learned here is that communication will make or break not only the project but the PM. It is critical to have the right amount and type of communication across the spectrum of Stakeholders involved in the project. Hold nothing back, especially if the project is slipping off the rails. A good PM will recognize this early, communicate the situation and find an acceptable remedy, all while gaining the respect and support of the project Sponsor.

Monitor and Control Risks

Be prepared. That is what this process is all about. Just like the Boy Scouts motto, Monitor and Control Risks is about keeping your finger on the pulse of the project and being prepared. Since the PM is continuously monitoring the risks, they will be prepared to handle them early and mitigate the impact.

The inputs are the Risk Register, because it contains the identified risks and any potential trouble areas. The Project Management Plan (and Risk Management Plan) is the plan for how the project is supposed to, and expected to, proceed. This is the ideal, the standard, for a perfect process. The Risk Management Plan details risks and the manner by which they are handled.

Work Performance Information also is bought in as an input. This is the current state of progress and is used to compare against the plan. This comparison will reveal what shape the process is in and whether any activities or work packages need attention.

Project Management. Simply Explained.

Organizational Process Assets also are inputs and in particular here we're looking for performance reports. These performance reports contain important information concerning HOW things got done, not WHAT got done. The salient information in the performance report concerns costs, time used and quality performance. These results are compared with the baselines to ensure that the project is on track against the plan.

Risk Reassessment is a continual process throughout the project. This is not to say that every risk is reevaluated continually. Some risks are identified and never materialize. There is no need to continuously monitor these. Other risks are always in danger and require almost constant monitoring. Risk audits are a tool used to help ensure that the risk process is functioning well and that the risks are monitored sufficiently. Risk Audits are an overview and do not drill down to individual risks, rather they are more concerned with the process or even categories of risks, ensuring proper care is taken to monitor these appropriately.

Variance and trend analysis is a tool that will allow the PM or Risk Manager to focus on trends that appear and variances that are outside acceptable limits, thereby triggering a response, requested attention or correction. Technical Performance Measurements also can be made on the process and activities. This is a focus on functionality and determining how the project met its goals for delivering the scope over time.

The Reserve Analysis should be included as an input because it should periodically be reviewed to ensure that a sufficient amount is held contingent to mitigate the current risk scenario.

Status meetings should include risk assessment and updates. This should be created as part of the culture of the Project Management team, holding status meetings and discussing risk, progress, lessons learned, etc.

The outputs from the Monitor and Control Risks process are Risk Register Updates and Organizational Process Updates. These two are self-explanatory. Any updates to the processes, documentation, etc., should be included in the appropriate register.

Change Requests may be an output if there are changes requested for any part of the process. The requests do not guarantee a change, rather the request is documented, along with the reason for the request. This becomes a permanent part of the project documentation and may be useful later in this project or in future projects.

Project Management Plan updates and Project Document updates, if any, also will be part of the outputs of this process.

Monitoring and Controlling Risk is all about being prepared, measuring current performance against planned performance, and requesting and

Douglas C. Ruh Jr.

making adjustments as necessary. These should be documented and become a permanent part of the project record. The reason for this (continual) process of monitor and control is to ensure that the project stays within scope, on budget, on time and that the Stakeholders are happy!

Administer Procurements

Administer Procurements happens after deciding which procurements are needed for the project. At this point the contractor and the PM review the contract and the work results that have been provided to ensure that the results of the contract work are in agreement with the results of the contractor's work.

If we ordered a white cake to be delivered on Saturday morning for our project and the contractor delivered a white and chocolate marble cake, the work results do not exactly match the contracted work. This may not make a huge difference on our cake project but what if we were rewiring a house? If the contract called for copper wiring and aluminum was installed, this could cause a fire down the road.

Typically the review will consist of comparing the results against the contract for the goods and services being delivered, on time, in sufficient quantities. Also, there may be additional items contained in the contract that should be reviewed, for example, delivery companies specified, delivery costs or terms may be included. The relationship between the parties also should be reviewed to ensure that a good working relationship is maintained and managed efficiently. This is important for the PM to maintain, since the contractor can make the project a success or cause unneeded difficulties during the project. It is also an advantage for the PM to maintain a good relationship so they may have an additional resource on future projects.

The PM's concern with, and dutiful maintenance of, the contract is necessary because the work performed can be considered another activity or work package. The same attention should be given to the contract results that would be normally given to any other activity in the project. The difference is that it has been hired out and because it has been hired out, there is less direct control over the process and the deliverable.

Administering Procurements is performed whenever goods or services are procured throughout the project, typically at predefined intervals specified by each contract. This does not prevent administering whenever there is a need or a request for administering.

The inputs that are needed for administering procurements are the Procurement Documents, which are the contracts that have been entered into. These outline in detail the agreement for performance of the deliverable. The Project Management Plan also is used as it is the overall plan for the project, including the procurements that are contracted. This is referred to frequently to ensure that the plan and the project are staying on track. Contracts also are part of the inputs. Performance reports are also brought into the process. They are a window into how the project is progressing. As we discussed earlier, a contract is really the same as an "off-campus" activity or work package, and must be managed in the same way as internal work.

Approved Change Requests is another input that is important to the process. Approved Change Requests include all change requests and in this instance, they refer to changes in the contract terms. Contract term changes are particularly important to monitor because they very often may result in litigation. They are a valid and binding contract between the two parties and should be seriously considered before they are approved and agreed to. Work Performance Information is invaluable because it informs the PM how the work is being conducted rather than how it is progressing against the schedule.

Although many organizations separate the project organization and process from the contract administration, the PM should still keep tabs on the contract administration, ensuring deliverables are obtained as expected.

So far, with all of this fancy language we can boil Administer Procurements down to its simplest term. It is simply the process of ensuring that the contracted work or deliverable is performed according to contracted terms. If there are changes, they will be agreed upon and a revised or amended contract will be agreed to.

To determine the performance of the contract, the PM has several tools at their disposal, including a Contract Change Control System, which ensures that any changes to the contracted design or performance is proposed, reviewed and approved. It helps with preventing little surprises at the end of the activity or project. Procurement Performance Reviews are periodic reviews of the progress made by the contracted company that review their progress against the contract and any other agreements that are included as part of the procurement agreement. Inspections and audits of the product are another tool that is used to ensure that the actual deliverable meets specifications.

Performance reporting, like the Earned Value Reporting that we touched on previously, is an excellent tool to help determine if the procurement is meeting expectations.

Payment or accounting systems also are good to have in place when measuring performance. This is useful especially when the contract has payment stipulations such as a payment of 10% to start and another payment of 20% when the project is 40% complete, or some other agreed upon milestone. Payment systems also are a good tool for ensuring only the work that is due to be paid gets paid. Avoiding duplicate payments also works toward Control Cost and makes the Sponsor happy.

Douglas C. Ruh Jr.

The output is the Procurement Documentation, which is a record of everything that went into the procurement process. Both parties, the buying and selling companies, keep these records. The contracts are only a small part of the documentation. Also included should be the supporting detail, accounting information, details on the deliverables, and whatever else could be seen as valuable to determine the success and performance of the agreement and the supplier. This information could be important in mid-stream in case their performance is not up to specifications and early termination of contract is considered. Also, at the end of the process, the supplier(s) can be evaluated and it can be decided if the supplier's performance is suitable to place them on a "trusted supplier" list or if they have gained special consideration for future work.

6 CLOSING A PROJECT

Close the Project or Phase

A project is an effort, duty or task that is short term or temporary, having a beginning and an end point that produces a specific, unique result.

A process is similar except that it has sustained results, it is repeated time and again, and is repetitive in nature.

Remember those lines? That's right! From the start of the book. Since this is a project, it has a definite ending point and we need to close the project down, making sure all loose ends are tied up to provide a date-definite end of the project. Enjoy the cake. We certainly do not want the project to sputter toward what is eventually considered an end. We want to define it, celebrate it, and then pick up and move to the next project.

To close this project we'll need the Project Management Plan, Accepted Deliverables, Organizational Process Assets and expert judgment.

To close the project, the PM will ensure that all activities on the Project Management Plan have been completed and all deliverables are completed. The Accepted Deliverables log will contain a listing of all accepted deliverables and any that were rejected, changed or scrapped. The accepted deliverables should be a match to the Project Management Plan, and the last incarnation of the baselines and deliverables expected. Once these are confirmed to have been handed off to the Sponsor, the PM will then turn their attention to the Organizational Process Assets. These are the tools built or bought for the project, any information or expertise gleaned from the project knowledge, experience that may have been gained and documented, and the proper documentation created throughout the project. This documentation will include information about deliverables, change logs, performance reports, templates or any other item that may serve the company in the future and is part of the work product of this project. The PM will then gather and deliver the updated Organizational Process Assets

Douglas C. Ruh Jr.

Register to the appropriate individual or group responsible for maintaining them.

We just went through the process for closing a project. It should be understood that this process is used for each phase of a project as well. If the project has 10 phases, then there will be 11 closing processes, 10 phase closing processes and one final project closing process.

Close Procurements

Close Procurements is just that - closing the procurements. There are certain duties that need to be performed to consider the procurement closed, including signing off on the finished work package or product, making final payments, formally ending the project through verbal and written acceptance of the deliverable, and acknowledging that the procurement is closed.

It is important to close out contracts to relieve the companies of any lingering questions or liabilities. The process provides both companies with a date-certain proof of closure, including ensuring that any claims are dealt with and satisfied. If there are claims open, then the procurement is not closed.

This closure applies to ALL procurements, even those that were not carried through to completion. If a supplier had to be terminated, there should be a closure process, explaining the date of release and reasons for release or termination of contract, if legally feasible to provide. This process not only closes the procurement, it is also a basic process for covering yourself that avoids dangling details at the end of the project.

The inputs for the Close Procurements process are the Project Management Plan and Procurement Documentation.

The Management Plan outlines the management of the project and activities, including procurements. The Project Documentation includes anything that was involved in the procurement, including the contact, performance reports, procurement inspections, payments made to the vendors and changes made to the contract. This information is necessary to determine lessons learned from the procurement experience and the performance of the contractor for future consideration.

Closing out a contract can be for one of three reasons, the first being success! The contract was entered into, the work performed and an acceptable deliverable was submitted within the contract parameters.

The second reason for closing out a contract is lack of performance. The supplier is simply not working to contracted expectations and the deliverable or work product is not up to contracted standards. The cost, time or quality (or all three) may be inadequate, thereby forcing the PM to cancel the contract and look for other means to complete the deliverable. In this case, there may need to be terms for breaking the contract negotiated. At other times the contract has a clause built in. Regardless, the break should be clean and clear, avoiding further entanglements that would prevent closing procurements.

The third reason is because the needs of the project have changed. This is a legitimate reason for closing procurements with the supplier. When this occurs, the PM should strive to make the break as amicable as possible with prompt payment for work already performed, sterling recommendations for the vendor or whatever else within reason needed to maintain a good relationship with the vendor.

The tool involved in the Closing Procurements process is Procurement Audits, which facilitate capturing the lessons learned from the contracting experience.

Negotiated settlements may be a tool that is necessary, especially if there are lingering items such as contract disputes for terms or performance that may call for negotiation or remediation. The goal is to have all loose ends tied up securely in order to close.

A Records Management System is used to archive the documents for future review and reference.

The output will include the Closed Procurements. These are the contracts that have been formally closed through a written notice and release of interest to the contracted company stating that the contract is completed and no longer in force. Essentially, it is a formal thank-you and handshake.

Organizational Process Assets Updates are included in the formal project archives. In other words, our lessons learned are detailed and archived with the project documentation for future review and use if needed.

Closing Thoughts

Not every aspect of Project Management will be needed for different projects that are encountered. The big takeaways for this author are that the entire detailed framework, though robust, is not always necessary. For instance, if you are constructing a building, most certainly all of the areas may be used, however, if a chef is creating a new menu for a restaurant, there may be a minimal amount of these tools used, for instance, if she is alone in creating the menu, there may be no need to develop the research and development team. The main points that I have learned is that preparation is essential. Know the project, study it before the actual hands-on work commences and decide what tools are most essential. Know the key stakeholders and keep necessary communication clear and robust. Manage the team members, time and materials effectively, gaining trust and buy-in for the project. There are various methods and tools available to perform these tasks. If there is enough time spent in preparation, the actual production should not have any exceptional difficulties. In preparation, the difficulties will have been thought through before they are encountered.

7 PMI AND PROFESSIONAL CERTIFICATIONS

The Project Management Institute (PMI)®, creator of the Project Management Book of Knowledge (PMBOK)® is a global industry standard bearer for project management.

PMI covers broad and diverse communities of practice and offer training, contacts and networking across many different areas, providing rich resources for expansion of knowledge, necessary educational credits, and subject matter experts and expertise.

Now to get to the nuts and bolts of the credentials that the PMI offers and what they mean.

The main certification process and schedule is the Project Management Professional, or PMP®. Individuals with the PMP designation lead and direct project teams. They are the lead person on the project. With the PMP, the individual would be expected to manage the entire project.

PMI also offers a certification called the CAPM®, or the Certified Associate of Project Management. This is a certification that designates the individual as a qualified member of the project team. This is someone who is capable of helping on a project or directing a phase, but not quite to the level of PMP. This could be considered a stepping stone to acquiring enough practical experience to become a PMP.

Three additional certifications are offered through the PMI organization, including the PgMP® or Program Management Professional. This is very similar to the PMP, however it is a much broader set of criteria and encompasses programs, not just projects. Programs (or portfolios) may

Douglas C. Ruh Jr.

contain many projects as a matter of course.

The remaining two certifications are specialized credentials, the PMI-SP® and the PMI-RMP®. The first, the PMI-SP is a certification for scheduling professionals. These individuals would show the proficiency to create and maintain project schedules. The PMI-RMP is a certification for the Risk Management Professional. These individuals would be specialists in identifying and mitigating risk in the project, thereby capitalizing on opportunity.

More information about the Project Management Institute can be obtained at their website, http://www.pmi.org/.

Project Management. Simply Explained.

ABOUT NORTHWEST UNIVERSITY

Northwest University is a regionally accredited university that is situated east of Seattle in the town of Kirkland, Washington since first opening it's doors in 1934. Northwest offers traditional and evening classes, awarding associate, baccalaureate, masters and doctorate degrees.
Northwest also offers the College of Adult & Professional Studies (CAPS) for students that have daytime commitments and also desire to obtain a degree. The CAPS program offers a variety of majors that allow the evening students to complete their education while still engaged in their daily responsibilities.

For more information about Northwest University please visit their website at www.northwestu.edu.

Project Management. Simply Explained.

www.ingramcontent.com/pod-product-compliance
Lightning Source LLC
Chambersburg PA
CBHW051736170526
45167CB00002B/963

* 9 7 8 1 4 9 9 6 2 2 5 0 8 *